Answers will vary for questions that require children to answer in their own words. Possible answers to most of these questions are given in *italics*.

Paper 1

1 The moon had shown itself.
2 Laurie's brother
3–5 *"our scarves were pearled with our breath"; "Hanging branches of willow, manacled in the ice"; "The dead sticks on the ground were easily seen, glittering with the night's new frost"; "We thought of caves, warm skins and fires"*
6–7 *When hands are very cold they take a while to feel warm again. Laurie knew they would get warm but was tormented by the pain until they did.*
8–9 *Laurie's mother is concerned, caring, sympathetic and loving, as illustrated in this line from the passage: "Then there were 'Where've-you-beens?', 'Never-minds', 'Oh-Dears', and 'Come-by-the-fire-you-look-half-dead'."*
10 Stroud
11–12 *because their voices were high-pitched, and they were speaking quickly about the dramatic events they had seen*
13 *Laurie's description of the heavy snowfall illustrates his love for it. "There were millions of tons of the lovely stuff, plastic, pure, all-purpose, which nobody owned, which one could carve or tunnel, eat, or just throw about."*
14 *gift, perk*
15 They are related to seasonal activities when money is given.
16 bounty
17 *They are the looks of people who have already given some money away and so don't have much left to give.*
18 *a reaction you don't have to think about, an impulse*
19–20 "Coming carol-barking then?" and "For a year we had praised the Lord out of key"
21 provisions
22 entrance
23 choice
24 advertisement
25 performance
26 bewilderment
27 destruction
28 applause
29 decorator
30 cellar
31 plumber
32 disaster
33 corridor
34 burglar
35 popular
36 circular
37 divisor
38 director
39 proprietor
40 partner
41–45 Dad said that **he was** going to mow the lawn. **He hoped** this **would be** the last time **he would** have to do it this year as **he was** tired of doing it.
46–47 They're, their
48–49 their, They're
50–51 There, there
52–53 There, their

54 they [illegible]
55 [illegible]
56 [illegible]
57 adjective
58 verb
59 noun
60 adverb
61–63 *lighthouse, firelight, sunlight*
64–66 *snowdrop, snowfall, snowball*
67–69 *daylight, daydream, daytime*
70 postage
71 sentence
72 parliament
73 machinery
74 fattening
75 mathematics
76 history
77–80 The men were cleaning their houses.
81–82 They jumped over the puddles.
83–86 They bought scarves to support their football teams.
87 principal
88 passed
89 rode
90 whose
91 waste
92 route
93 prey
94 to
95 course
96–100 Sam was caught, thank goodness, otherwise I would have been blamed for stealing the sweets, pen, magazine, Harry Potter book and racing car.

Paper 2

1 seventy miles per hour
2 left wing
3 two thousand feet
4 *amazing, determined, huge*
5 *the difference between having and then losing control of his situation*
6 because travelling at the speed Jonathan was, to crash into the sea was like hitting a wall of bricks
7–8 "the weight of failure was even heavier on his back" and "drag him gently down to the bottom, and end it all."
9 *from now on*
10 falcon
11 "I am limited by my nature" or "as a poor limited seagull"
12–13 *Jonathan was not alert to listen to the hollow voice because he was so tied up in his own thoughts, taking in the new experience. This is shown in*

the line "The moon and the lights twinkling on the water ...".

14 because their sight isn't equipped for night flying; their brains aren't made to make night flying easy or safe

15 because he realised that the solution to his problem was that he needed short wings like a falcon; because he had just solved his problem

16–17 because Jonathan looked grey under the moonlight and he was travelling at a tremendous speed like a cannonball

18–20 a description that might include the following words or ideas: focused, determined, perfectionist, content, assured, confident, different, striving, wants to be better than others, wants to stretch himself as much as possible, wants to be the first to do something different/difficult, stubborn, arrogant

21 mice
22 stories
23 cargoes or cargos
24 thieves
25 trolleys
26 potatoes
27 gases
28 oxen
29 roofs
30 valleys
31 6
32 4
33 3
34 1
35 5
36 2
37–46 cook, crutch, lanyard, wedge, movement, ashore, heaviest, deck, spaces, walk
47 two peas
48 bat
49 cucumber
50 pie
51 gold
52 lead
53 cricket
54 hatter
55 Ian had a large appetite.
56 Rachel wrote the invitations to her party neatly.
57 She intently watched the TV programme.
58 Softly she sang the lilting tune.
59 They got up early on Sunday.
60–61 He lifted the kitten carefully and put it in the basket.
62 expand
63 export
64 decrease
65 coarse, thick
66 free
67 permanent
68 inferior
69 accept, agree
70 singular
71 create
72 crept
73 lost
74 spoke
75 rang
76 broke
77–83 They jumped into the car before it sped off at high speed. Joseph whispered that his mum had never been so cross. She reminded him of a bull! They agreed with him.
84–88 "What about the horse? You don't mention sending that back," said Thorin.
89–91 [3 words, each with the prefix 'dis' – e.g. disloyal, discontinue, displease]
92–94 [3 words, each with the prefix 'mis' – e.g. misunderstand, mislead, misplace]
95 adjective
96 noun
97 verb
98 adverb
99 verb
100 adjective

Paper 3

1 a snake
2 straight
3 in the way the snake looked at/acknowledged the onlooker
4 during the day
5–7 mused – pondered
venomous – poisonous
perversity – strangeness; opposite of what is expected/acceptable
8 'On the day of Sicilian July, with Etna smoking' or 'For in Sicily the black, black snakes are innocent, the gold are venomous.'
9 soft-bellied; two-forked tongue; flickered his tongue like a forked night
10 The onlooker felt honoured because the snake had chosen his water trough to drink from.
11 The earth is described as 'secret' as it is unknown to the onlooker. It is the snake's domain.
12–13 The onlooker feels scared, is confused about his/her feelings about the snake, although has great respect for it. "And yet those voices: If you were not afraid, you would kill him!"; "And truly I was afraid, I was most afraid, But even so, honoured still more".
14–15 The snake is relaxed, unhurried: "He drank enough and lifted his head, dreamily, as one who has drunken"; "And slowly turned his head"; "And slowly, very slowly, as if thrice adream, proceeded to draw his slow length curving round".
16 The log is described as 'clumsy' because logs aren't easy objects to throw with precision and speed.
17 The onlooker threw the log as she/he felt braver with the snake's back turned; for a brief second the onlooker wanted to show the snake that she/he was mightier than it; the onlooker gave in to what she/he had been taught about snakes being seen as dangerous and needing to be killed.
18–19 hot, dry, "On a hot, hot day, and I in pyjamas for the heat"; "from the burning bowels of the earth"

20 *The main point is that one shouldn't always give way to what one has been told, but question actions before participating in them.*

21–27 athlete, student, friend, typist, knitter, child, cat
28 north east
29 public limited company
30 please turn over
31 department
32 milligram(s)
33 British Summer Time or British Standard Time
34 United Kingdom
35 for
36 in
37 on
38 on
39 for
40 at
41 by
42 up
43 foreign
44 believe
45 achieve
46 conceited
47 neighbour
48 audience
49 height
50 ceiling
51 badly
52 slither
53 quantity
54 woollen
55 where
56 ugly
57 but
58–59 *helpful, helping*
60–61 *return, returned*
62–63 *collection, collectable*
64–65 *reasonable, unreasonable*
66–67 *[2 words with the root word 'agree' – e.g. agreeable, disagree]*
68–76 Egyptian, David, February, Wales, Denmark, June, Manchester, Tuesday, Britney *[note: queen is an incorrect answer as its capitalisation is dependent on context]*
77 February
78 tomorrow
79 possess
80 government
81 punishment
82 fragrance
83 arrival
84 length
85 conclusion
86 assistance
87 Gina didn't swim in the sea.
88 There weren't any stars out tonight or There were no stars out tonight.
89 The dogs didn't wait.
90 The playground wasn't open.
91 Caroline didn't want to/a ride in the car.
92 Raj's family hadn't won any money on the lottery or Raj's family had won no money on the lottery.

93–100 *[8 answers from] you're, you've, won't, they'll, they've, haven't, they're, you'll, aren't*

Paper 4

1 pick and freeze vegetables and fruits
2 *wants to but hasn't yet started; deciding whether to do something or not*
3–5 bad for the environment to use the car to get to the shops; the methods used to grow the vegetables can't be controlled; the price you have to pay is fixed by the supermarkets; the freshness is decided by how supermarkets stack/shelve the produce
6 carrot
7 those who already grow their own vegetables
8 easy
9–11 *earth for nutrients, seeds to grow, sunshine, water – to provide the right conditions for the seed to become a plant*
12 *a laid back, relaxed, non-interfering way of growing*
13 *settling for the best in the surroundings available*
14 because they need cutting down to provide light for the vegetable patch
15–17 "When you buy your vegetables, you are a slave"; his description of the grown carrot, "They are sleek, pointed, orange miracles …"; his conviction that "As I said earlier, growing vegetables is easy."
18–20 *planning where the vegetables will grow, choosing a suitable range of vegetables, preparing the soil for planting, buying seeds, buying garden equipment*
21–23 *purr, chug, throb*
24–26 *howl, whoosh, whistle*
27–29 *plop, gurgle, splash*
30 *swimming, swimmer*
31 *experimental, experimented*
32 *useful, user*
33 *excitable, excitement*
34 *thoughtless, thoughtful*
35 *childhood, children*
36 *marriage, married*
37 *excellence, excellent*
38 *boredom, bored*
39 *See you later.*
40 *You're making fun of me!*
41 *Did you take the day off school?*
42 *It was a very good concert.*
43 *You look good in those sunglasses.*
44 The following children are absent today: Amina, Ilesh, Frank, Michael and Fayza.
45 The school magazine reported: No school uniform for a day!
46 An eyewitness stated: The car turned over as it crashed into the tree, just missing three people …
47 The following classes are out on a school trip today: Class 6L, Class 6T and Class 6M.
48 The local paper reported: School flooded, children sent home.
49 elegant
50 prudent
51 adjacent
52 abundant

53 arrogant
54 extravagant
55 continent
56 immigrant
57 cement
58–64 gosling, statuette, droplet, hamlet, duckling, starlet, majorette
65 the rabbit's food
66 Leanne's hairbrush
67 the players' football
68 the museum's café
69 a bicycle's handlebar
70 Mr Dodd's newspaper
71 author or writer
72 stationery
73 apologised
74 recently or lately
75 present
76 unnecessary or pointless or futile
77–85 [words with the correct number of syllables]
86–100 "I will buy you some new shoes," said Mum, "but not until you have out–grown the ones you are wearing now."
"But these aren't fashionable," complained Sam. "Nobody has shoes like these now."
Mum just laughed.

Paper 5

1 while working as a Mississippi river pilot; from the term used to mean two fathoms; from the term used to mean that the water was deep enough for it to be safe to sail along
2 *A person who has been driven out of a group or rejected by society.*
3 Cairo
4 Jim
5 the second
6 when Huckleberry Finn ties the boat to some saplings but the current pulls the saplings out
7–8 "you couldn't see twenty yards" and "solid white fog"
9–10 scared – *because in the hostile conditions he had to find Jim*
excited – *because of the difficult conditions and the speed he had to work at in order to track down Jim*
11 because he was in some kind of trouble and at night he couldn't be spotted so easily
12 *'hollering'* or *'whooped'*
13 He was frightened that he would run into something.
14–16 the darkness, the fog and the strength of the current
17 *When in fog your senses are confused as you can't see as well, so things can look and sound strange.*
18–20 an account of Huckleberry Finn's character using evidence from the passage to support the answer; *vulnerable "it made me so sick and scared", resourceful "We would sell the raft", relatively calm, determined*
21 *recklessly*
22 *greedily*
23 *brilliantly*

24 *vaguely*
25 *attentively*
26 *neatly*
27 *bravely*
28 *carefully*
29–30 inquiry; enquiry
31–32 formally; formerly
33–34 beech, beach
35 3
36 5
37 7
38 6
39 1
40 4
41 2
42 unlock
43 impolite
44 disagree
45 incapable
46 irregular
47 disown
48 unreliable
49–51 The mouse lived in the old barn until the child found it.
52–54 The class lined up quietly once its teacher had arrived.
55–59 The satsuma was eaten quickly by the child, who then wanted a chocolate!
60 transfusion
61 transfuse
62 transformer
63 transfigure
64 transference
65 transfer
66–75 "What time are you going home?" said Jill to her brother. "I don't want to be late."
Tim replied, "I'll go when you are ready."
76–87 [*a clause, a section of a sentence with a verb (one mark) using a different connective each time (one mark)*]
88 salmon
89 wife
90 opportunity
91 matrix
92 cactus
93 solo
94 appendix
95 puppy
96 blanket
97 veil of darkness
98 soft cushion
99 cotton wool
100 shimmering river

Paper 6

1 at night
2 the road
3 deep red, claret
4 2
5 *It describes the stars twinkling in the sky like jewels.*

A4

6–8 *amount of wealth, intelligence, cleanliness, confidence, speaking ability*

9 *because dogs can't speak and in that situation Tim couldn't either*

10–11 The Highwayman was after people's money: "But I shall be back with the yellow gold before the morning light."

12 protectors of the law/law enforcement

13–15 *caring about her appearance, beautiful, black-haired, in love, enjoying excitement/risk, interested in the well-dressed Highwayman, prepared to wait*

16 one that tells a story

17–20 *the way The Highwayman approaches the inn-door; the description of what he looks like; the way he whistled a tune at the landlord's daughter's window; the way he talks to the landlord's daughter and gallops off*

21 ran

22 cassette

23 large

24 cried

25 quickly

26 she

27 loveable or lovable

28 useful or useable or usable

29 plentiful

30 wonderful

31 valuable

32 laughable

33 rightful or rightable

34 powerful

35 workable

36–45

Synonyms	Antonyms
vacant/empty	absence/presence
tranquil/peaceful	here/there
option/choice	coarse/fine
famous/noted	seldom/often
caution/care	few/many

46–52 visitor, worker, editor, relation, adult, pupil, passenger

53–54 One morning, as the sun was rising, Jack crept out of the house.

55 In his hand was a small bag, just large enough to carry an apple, two sandwiches and a big slice of cake.

56–57 He turned, looked towards the house, then ran across the field.

58 Jack moved slowly, worried he might be seen.

59–61 As he entered the cave, his eyes adjusting to the darkness, he recognised the silhouette of Aimee, his young and vulnerable sister.

62 business

63 imaginary

64 conscience

65 environment

66 miscellaneous

67 persuasion

68 stomach

69 necessary

70 possession

71 sequence

72 five tigers' tails

73 nine cows' calves

74 three men's suits

75 four gates' hinges

76 one dog's bone

77 cm

78 kg

79 l

80 mm

81 sq.

82 e.g.

83 no.

84 i.e.

85 I was pleased when the film, <u>frightening and full of suspense</u>, was over!

86 The morning snow, <u>beautiful but cold</u>, had settled outside my bedroom window.

87 The wild horse, <u>dappled grey with a tangled mane</u>, drank silently at the water's edge.

88 Last night's homework, <u>confusing and difficult</u>, took Nina many hours to complete.

89 Our local swimming pool, <u>green, murky and a little smelly</u>, hadn't been cleaned recently.

90 Ben, <u>strong and athletic</u>, was a capable athlete.

91 1

92 3

93 2

94 2

95 3

96 1

97 Capital punishment no longer takes place in Great Britain; it is still used in America.

98 Helen loves doing homework; Laura prefers to socialise.

99 We visited the crown jewels; jewels indeed fit for a queen.

100 An art gallery in London has a collection of Monet pictures; an exhibition which is simply too good to miss.

Paper 7

1 Buckinghamshire

2 Dahl's wife/widow

3–4 the chocolate doors and foil ball of chocolate wrappers

5 *because it is a very modern museum that uses the latest technology and celebrates children getting involved*

6 Boy

7 *because it might remind them of their school days*

8 in the 1970s

9 *Dahl is saying to those that cast aside the possibilities of magic that unless they open their minds to it they will never know if it is possible or not.*

10–11 *A visit to the toilet at this museum is accompanied with loud sounds and Dahl's voice saying "I will not eat worms!"*

12 *The reporter describes Dahl as 'the great man' as he is known to be one of the greatest children's authors of his generation.*

13 large buildings

14–16 Roald Dahl would approve of this museum because it appeals to children's imaginations, it is state-of-the-art, and it is interactive. Evidence from the article: *"it's the BFG's dream bottle in the centre of the room that has children flocking"; "Everything is designed to be opened and closed, twiddled and fiddled"; "you acted out the stories too, and that was really funny."*

17–18 [child's own description of the type of person Dahl was, e.g. *fun, strange, imaginative, hardworking, wise etc. Evidence taken from the article to support their answer*]

19–20 *parents/people who want to know about places they can take children, because the article explains what types of activity are there for children*

21 rain
22 tried
23 slept
24 felt
25 saw
26 found
27 met
28 built
29 began
30 The teachers' cars
31 My cousin's cat
32 The children's umbrellas
33 The woman's bank account
34 The singers' guitars
35 The dentist's chair
36 The flats' walls
37–38 water – *splash, plop*
39–40 a volcano – *whoosh, gurgle, roar*
41–42 a tree – *crack, rustle*
43 *over*
44 *with*
45 *from*
46 *along*
47 *under*
48 *above*
49 *by*
50 *for*
51 signify
52 happy
53 duty
54 prestige
55 heavy
56 date
57 depend
58 confess
59–69 Saturday, Obedience, remain, owners, several, toy, terriers, hounds, judges, animals, prizes
70 is
71 have
72 is
73 are
74 is
75 are
76 Welsh
77 Tibetan
78 Dutch
79 Portuguese

80–92 Jacob was beginning to get worried; he hadn't heard them for at least five minutes. Jacob called "Is that you, Sandy? Please answer if it is."
"Of course it is! Who else would it be?" responded Sandy, giggling.
(or "Of course it is. ...")

93–100 [completion of the table with words with the correct number of syllables]

Paper 8

1 Land of Everlasting Winter
2 a giant eagle
3 Gudrun
4 a piece of dark
5 Cark!
6 No Man's Land
7 *The kingdom no longer has any dark, hence there is no night to ride through.*
8–9 *Gudrun felt comforted (she saw familiar faces), tired (she began to become sleepy) and entranced (she forgot what she had come for).*
10 *Houniman meant that whether they could get dark from No Man's Land or not it was too dangerous to stay there. They would have to look elsewhere.*
11 *The story was titled 'The Cost of Night' because the people of King Merrion's kingdom realised how important night was to them.*
12–15 Lord of Winter – *giant eagle, grumpy, angry, cold* old woman – *hungry, grumpy, bad-tempered* uncle poet – *focused on task, absent-minded* All three seem unhappy, not content.
16–20 animals in the story speak and act as humans; concept of dark as something that can be taken by someone; magical/unreal events presented as if common happenings; the poet is able to draw out mist like long threads; land where words freeze
21 adhere
22 accelerate
23 abandon or abscond
24 acute
25 alter or alteration
26 abundant
27 abbreviate or abridge
28 attempt
29–40

Nouns	Verbs	Adjectives
reality	expect	carefree
uncertainty	caught	happy
energy	drown	foolish
sunlight	met	artificial

41 impatient
42 illegible
43 irresponsible
44 discontented
45 uninformed, misinformed
46 nonsense
47 inconsiderate
48 uncertain

49–55 As the water trickled off the roof, on to the path and down into the ever increasing stream, Mark wished it would stop raining. Usually a patient boy, he wouldn't have minded being trapped in the club house if he wasn't supposed to have been home ages ago. Mark had left with Tony, Matt, Anil and Rick but had to return as he had forgotten, in all the excitement, his football kit.

56 dynasties
57 surveys
58 frequencies
59 injuries
60 galleries
61 melodies
62 anthologies
63 photocopies

64–66 The young cat, full of fun, killed the mouse; Dad was pleased.

67 The aircraft was nearly empty; empty seats are good for passengers but bad news for airlines.

68 Polar bears are beginning to move closer to people's homes; it can't be long before there is an attack.

69–71 Rugby training is hard work; we start with a run, continue with 30 press-ups, practise moves and finish with a training match.

72 active
73 active
74 passive
75 active
76 passive

77–82 [answers each describing the metaphors]
83 silently
84 prison
85 dictionary
86 nursery
87 company
88 chocolate
89 different
90 fragrance
91 temperature

92–94 [each sentence completed as a conditional sentence. A conditional sentence is a sentence that expresses the idea that one thing depends on something else e.g. *Sundeep will go to the shop or he won't have any bread for lunch tomorrow.*]

95 better
96 latest
97 worse
98 least
99–100 harder, cleverer

Paper 9

1 "occasions of great public rejoicing"
2 three months
3 basin/porringer
4 to catch any stray splashes of gruel
5 *They held a meeting.*
6–7 *One boy suggested he might eat the boy that slept next to him, he was so hungry. Oliver was chosen at random, 'lots were cast'.*

8 *He was so miserable and hungry that he would risk anything for some more food.*
9 *extreme boldness*
10 *It emphasises the difference between him and the thin, ill, starving boys.*
11–13 *Mr Bumble's violence is illustrated when hitting out at Oliver when he asked for more, etc.*
14–15 [child's description of the room in which Oliver was imprisoned: *dark, gloomy, cold, bare, etc.*]
16 hang himself
17–18 [child's reaction to the final sentence of the passage: *the last sentence makes me feel sad and worried for Oliver because he is desperate for someone to love and take care of him. This is shown when he tries to curl up to the wall, wanting someone to protect and help him.*]
19–20 *The punishment seems excessive for the crime of asking for more food. It suggests that those in charge of the boys were actually afraid of them and needed to keep them in such a way that they ruled them by fear; those in charge had little feeling for the boys or for the fact that they were only children.*

21 anxious
22 perilous
23 regional
24 choral
25 methodical
26 long
27 ornamental
28 metallic
29 duck's back
30 china shop
31 fiddle
32 March hare or hatter or coot
33 church mouse
34 dodo or doornail
35 sauce
36 altar
37 source
38 practice
39 stationary
40 practise
41 alter
42 desert
43 stationery
44 dessert

45–50 [a clause (a section of a sentence with a verb) added to each of the sentences, e.g. *My friend knows more about horses than I do, which is a good thing since she lives on a farm.*]

51 has
52 should
53 comes
54 here
55 are
56 will
57 says
58 shall
59 the cat's tail
60 the five children's coats
61 the apple's pips or the apples' pips
62 the three dogs' bones

63 the seven houses' keys
64 the video's case
65 the four horses' foals
66 the six computers' keyboards
67 herd
68 plague or swarm
69 pride
70 band or group
71 litter
72 flock
73 murder
74–81 engagement, alignment, membership, receivership, censorship, scholarship, enhancement, contentment
82–96 It was **S**unday afternoon, the sun was glinting through the trees and it was warm**.** **A**melia called to **G**eorge, **"A**re we going to do something today**?** **I**'m bored of just sitting here**."** **H**e ignored her**.**
97–100 [a mnemonic (a way of remembering a particular spelling) for each of the four words listed, e.g. WEIGHT – W plus eight]

Paper 10

1 Princess Beatrice
2 in her sitting-room at Kensington Palace
3 uncle
4–5 desirous – *wanting, having a desire, desiring* condolence – *sympathy*
6–7 *pleased, proud, determined, excited*
8–9 *She would have expressed her sympathy and her fondness for her uncle. Evidence from the extract: "whom I charged to express my feelings of condolence and sorrow to the poor Queen".*
10 1 year and 8 days.
11–12 the nerves and excitement of the day ahead
13 because the crown was about to be placed on her head
14 *Victoria described herself as loaded as at this point she was wearing and holding all the required articles for the Coronation.*
15 Dalmatic robe
16–17 *In those days television hadn't been invented, so to watch and be part of such an important occasion people had to actually attend; people would want to be a part of an historic event; people wanted to see the new Queen; people wanted to show the new Queen that they supported her.*
18–20 evidence from the extract highlighting how Victoria felt at her Coronation: *"shall ever remember this day as the proudest of my life"*
21–22 <u>censure</u> **praise**
23–24 <u>raise</u> **lower**
25–26 <u>gather</u> **disperse**
27–28 <u>increase</u> **contract**
29–30 <u>minimum</u> **most**
31 whether

32 until
33 unless
34 because
35 r**h**ythm
36 rei**g**n
37 **k**not
38 r**h**ombus
39 colum**n**
40 **h**our
41 hym**n**
42 **g**uard
43 active
44 passive
45 active
46 active
47 active
48 passive
49 passive
50 3
51 6
52 5
53 2
54 7
55 8
56 1
57 4
58–65 [words in bold used in both a statement (a formal account of facts) and then a question]
66–67 far off   e.g. *television*
68–69 small or millionth   e.g. *microphone* or *micrometre*
70–71 below or under   e.g. *submerge*
72–73 water   e.g. *aquamarine*
74–75 self   e.g. *autograph*
76 from
77 on
78 to
79 beyond
80 on
81 outside
82 up
83–86 [four sentences, each with a colon (a colon is used to show that what follows is an example quotation, list or summary of what precedes it).]
87 fought
88 built
89 ran
90 got
91 meant
92 became
93 found
94 felt
95 interesting
96 unfortunately
97 specification
98 infrastructure
99 rehearsal
100 independence

Bond

New Edition

Assessment Papers

Fifth papers in English

J M Bond
and Sarah Lindsay

Nelson Thornes

First published in 1988 as Further Fourth Assessment Papers in English by:
Thomas Nelson Ltd

This edition published in 2007 by:
Nelson Thornes Ltd
Delta Place
27 Bath Road
CHELTENHAM
GL53 7TH
United Kingdom

08 09 10 11 / 10 9 8 7 6 5 4 3

A catalogue record for this book is available from the British Library

ISBN 978 0 7487 8483 7

Illustrations by Nigel Kitching
Page make-up by GreenGate Publishing Services, Tonbridge, Kent

Printed and bound in Croatia by Zrinski

Acknowledgements

The authors and publishers wish to thank the following for permission to use copyright material:

extract from *Cider with Rosie* by Laurie Lee, published by Hogarth Press. Reprinted by permission of The Random House Group Ltd; extract from *Jonathan Livingston Seagull: A Story* by Richard Bach, reprinted by permission of HarperCollins Publishers Ltd; extract from *The River Cottage Cookbook* by Hugh Fearnley-Whittingstall, reprinted by permission of HarperCollins Publishers Ltd; extract from *The Highwayman* by Alfred Noyes, reprinted by permission of The Society of Authors as the Literary Representative of the estate of Alfred Noyes; extract from Times Online *A Dahl of a day out* by Damian Kelleher / NI Syndication Ltd, 2006; extract from *A Small Pinch of Weather* 'The Cost of Night' by Joan Aiken, reprinted by permission of Lutterworth Press.

Every effort has been made to trace the copyright holders, but if any have been inadvertently overlooked the publishers will be pleased to make the necessary arrangement at the first opportunity.

Before you get started

What is Bond?

This book is part of the Bond Assessment Papers series for English, which provides **thorough and continuous practice of key English skills** from ages five to thirteen. Bond's English resources are ideal preparation for many different kinds of tests and exams – from SATs to 11+ and other secondary school selection exams.

How does the scope of this book match real exam content?

Fifth and *More Fifth Papers* are the advanced Bond 11+ books. Each paper is **pitched a level above a typical 11+ exam**, providing greater challenge and stretching skills further. The papers practise comprehension, spelling, grammar and vocabulary work. They are also in line with other selective exams for this age group. The coverage is matched to the National Curriculum and the National Literacy Strategy and will also **provide invaluable preparation for higher level Key Stage 2 SATs performance**. It is outside the scope of this book to practise extended and creative writing skills. *Bond The Secrets of 11+ Writing* provides full coverage of writing skills.

What does the book contain?

- **10 papers** – each one contains 100 questions.

- **Tutorial links throughout** – 📖 – this icon appears in the margin next to the questions. It indicates links to the relevant section in *How to do 11+ English*, our invaluable subject guide that offers explanations and practice for all core question types.

- **Scoring devices** – there are score boxes in the margins and a Progress Chart on page 64. The chart is a visual and motivating way for children to see how they are doing. It also turns the score into a percentage that can help decide what to do next.

- **Next Step Planner** – advice on what to do after finishing the papers can be found on the inside back cover.

- **Answers** – located in an easily-removed central pull-out section. If you lose your answers, please email cservices@nelsonthornes.com for another copy.

How can you use this book?

One of the great strengths of Bond Assessment Papers is their flexibility. They can be used at home, in school and by tutors to:

- set **timed formal practice tests** – allow about 50 minutes per paper in line with standard 11+ demands. Reduce the suggested time limit by five minutes to practise working at speed.

- provide **bite-sized chunks** for regular practice

- **highlight strengths and weaknesses** in the core skills

- identify **individual needs**

- set **homework**

- follow a **complete 11+ preparation strategy** alongside *The Parents' Stress-free Guide to the 11+* (see below).

It is best to start at the beginning and work though the papers in order. If you are using the book as part of a careful run in to the 11+, we suggest that you also have four other essential Bond resources close at hand:

How to do 11+ English: the subject guide that explains all the question types practised in this book. Use the cross-reference icons to find the relevant sections.

The Secrets of 11+ Comprehension: the practical handbook that clearly shows children how to read and understand the text, understand the questions and assess their own answers.

The Secrets of 11+ Writing: the essential resource that explains the key components of successful writing.

The Parents' Stress-free Guide to the 11+: the step-by-step guide to the whole 11+ experience. It clearly explains the 11+ process, provides guidance on how to assess children, helps you to set complete action plans for practice and explains how you can use the *Fifth* and *More Fifth Papers in English* as part of a strategic run-in to the exam.

See the inside front cover for more details of these books.

What does a score mean and how can it be improved?

It is unfortunately impossible to guarantee that a child will pass the 11+ exam if they achieve a certain score on any practice book or paper. Success on the day depends on a host of factors, including the scores of the other children sitting the test. However, we can give some guidance on what a score indicates and how to improve it.

If children colour in the Progress Chart on page 64, this will give an idea of present performance in percentage terms. The Next Step Planner inside the back cover will help you to decide what to do next to help a child progress. It is always valuable to go over wrong answers with children. If they are having trouble with any particular question type, follow the tutorial links to *How to do 11+ English* for step-by-step explanations and further practice.

Don't forget the website…!

Visit www.assessmentpapers.co.uk for lots of advice, information and suggestions on everything to do with Bond, the 11+ and helping children to do their best.

Key words

Some special words are used in this book. You will find them in **bold** each time they appear in the Papers. These words are explained here.

abbreviation   a word or words which is/are shortened

active verb   when the main person or thing does the action   *he took it*

adjective   a word that describes somebody or something

adjectival phrase   a group of words describing a noun

adverb   a word that gives extra meaning to a verb

alphabetical order   words arranged in the order found in the alphabet

antonym   a word with a meaning opposite to another word   *hot – cold*

clause   a section of a sentence with a verb

collective noun   a word referring to a group   *swarm*

compound word   a word made up of two other words   *football*

conditional   a clause or sentence expressing the idea that one thing depends on something else

conjunction   a word used to link sentences, phrases or words   *and, but*

connective   a word or words that joins clauses or sentences

contraction   two words shortened into one with an apostrophe placed where the letter/s have been dropped   *do not = don't*

definition   a meaning of a word

diminutive   a word implying smallness   *booklet*

homophone   a word that has the same sound as another but a different meaning or spelling   *right/write*

infinitive   the base form of a verb without any additional endings   *clap*

metaphor   an expression in which something is described in terms usually associated with another *the sky is a sapphire sea*

mnemonic   a device to learn particular spellings   *There is a rat in separate*

noun   a word for somebody or something

onomatopoeic   a word that echoes a sound, associated with its meaning   *hiss*

passive verb   when the main person or thing has the action done to it *it was taken by him*

past tense   form of a verb showing that something has already happened

phrase   a group of words that act as a unit

plural   more than one   *cats*

prefix   a group of letters added to the beginning of a word   *un, dis*

preposition   a word that relates other words to each other   *the book on the table*

pronoun   a word used to replace a noun   *them*

root word   a word to which prefixes or suffixes can be added to make other words   *quickly*

sentence   a unit of written language which makes sense by itself

simile   an expression to describe what something is like   *as cold as ice*

singular   one   *cat*

suffix   a group of letters added to the end of a word   *ly, ful*

superlative   describes the limit of a quality (adjective or adverb)   *most/least* or *shortest*

synonym   a word with the same or very similar meaning as another word   *quick – fast*

verb   a 'doing' or 'being' word

The author, Laurie Lee, wrote this book about his childhood memories.

The frozen pond on such a winter's evening was a very treadmill of pleasure. Time
was uncounted; we played ourselves into exhaustion. We ran and slid till we dripped
with sweat; our scarves were pearled with our breath. The reeds and horse-tails at
the pond's edge smelt as pungent as old men's fingers. Hanging branches of willow,
manacled in the ice, bloomed like lilac in the setting sun. Then the frost moon rose   5
through the charcoal trees and we knew that we'd played too long.

We had promised Mother we would fetch some wood. We had to get some each
day in winter. Jack and I, hands in pockets, mooched silently up the lane; it was
night now, and we were frightened. The beech wood was a cavern of moonlight and
shadows, and we kept very close together.   10

The dead sticks on the ground were easily seen, glittering with the night's new
frost. As we ripped them from the earth, scabbed with soil and leaves, our hands
began to burn with the cold. The wood was silent and freezing hard, white and
smelling of wolves. Such a night as lost hunters must have stared upon when first
they wandered north into the Ice Age. We thought of caves, warm skins and fires,   15
grabbed our sticks, and tore off home.

Then there were 'Where've-you-beens?', 'Never-minds', 'Oh-Dears', and 'Come-
by-the-fire-you-look-half-dead'. First the long slow torment as our hands thawed out,
a quiet agony of returning blood. Worse than toothache it was; I sat there sobbing,
but gradually the pain wave passed. Then we had jugs of tea, hot toast and dripping; 20
and later our sisters came. 'It was murder in Stroud. I fell down twice – in the High
Street – and tore my stockings. I'm sure I showed everything. It was terrible, Ma.
And a horse went through Maypole's window. And old Mr Fowler couldn't get down
the hill and had to sit on his bottom and slide. It's freezing harder than ever now.
We won't none of us be able to budge tomorrow.'   25

They sat at their tea and went on talking about it in their sing-song disaster voices. And we boys were content to know the winter had come, total winter, the new occupation… .

Later, towards Christmas, there was heavy snow, which raised the roads to the tops of the hedges. There were millions of tons of the lovely stuff, plastic, pure, all-purpose, which nobody owned, which one could carve or tunnel, eat, or just throw about. It covered the hills and cut off the villages, but nobody thought of rescues; for there was hay in the barns and flour in the kitchens, the women baked bread, the cattle were fed and sheltered – we'd been cut off before, after all.   30

The week before Christmas, when the snow seemed to lie thickest, was the moment for carol-singing; and when I think back to those nights it is to the crunch of snow and to the lights of the lanterns on it. Carol-singing in my village was a special tithe for the boys; the girls had little to do with it. Like hay-making, blackberrying, stone-clearing, and wishing-people-a-happy-Easter, it was one of our seasonal perks.   35

By instinct we knew just when to begin it; a day too soon and we should have been unwelcome, a day too late and we should have received lean looks from people whose bounty was already exhausted. When the true moment came, exactly balanced, we recognised it and were ready.   40

So as soon as the wood had been stacked in the oven to dry for the morning fire, we put on our scarves and went out through the streets, calling loudly between our hands, till the various boys who knew the signal ran out from their houses to join us.   45

One by one they came stumbling over the snow, swinging their lanterns around their heads, shouting and coughing horribly.

'Coming carol-barking then?'

We were the Church Choir, so no answer was necessary. For a year we had praised the Lord out of key, and as a reward for this service – on top of the Outing – we now had the right to visit all the big houses, to sing our carols and collect our tribute.   50

To work them all meant a five-mile foot journey over wild and generally snowed-up country. So the first thing we did was to plan our route; a formality, as the route never changed. All the same, we blew on our fingers and argued; and then we chose our Leader. This was not binding, for we all fancied ourselves as Leaders, and he who started the night in that position usually trailed home with a bloody nose.   55

From *Cider with Rosie* by Laurie Lee

Answer these questions.

1 How did Laurie know he had played too long?

The moon had shown itself 6K

Laurie knew he had Played too long because it was night

2 What relation is Jack to the writer?

Jack is Laurie lee in his childhood ✗ His brother

9:30—10:11 not including checking

3

3–5 Find three pieces of evidence from the passage that convey to the reader how cold it is on this winter's evening.

our hands began to burn with cold.
The wood was solid and freezing had
The Ice Age

6–7 Explain why the thawing of Laurie's hands is described as a 'long slow torment' (line 18).

because it hurt alot and was a bit
like torture. It was probably a fast
process but felt slow

8–9 Using evidence from the passage, describe Laurie's mother.

Lauries mother was very reliant
on jack. She was also quiet quite
kind

10 Which town did Laurie live near? _____ ?

11–12 Why are Laurie's sisters described as having 'sing-song disaster voices' (line 26)?

because they cannot sing and
Jack does not like it.

13 What evidence is there in the passage that indicates Laurie's love of the snow?

we played ourselves into exhaustion

14 A tithe was a tax. What do you think it means in this passage (line 38)?

tax for the boys

15 Why, on line 39, are the activities listed seen as 'seasonal perks'?

because they are seasonal

16 Which word, in the paragraphs describing the carol singing, means generosity?

key

17 Why does Laurie describe the faces of people as having 'lean looks' if they arrived a day too late (line 41)?

because they already would have had sin

4

18 What does 'instinct' mean (line 40)?

by mind ✗

19–20 Which two **phrases** in the passage suggest the Church Choir wasn't very good?

They blew on there singers and argued so no answer was necessary ✗

~~4~~ 20

D 6

Form a **noun** from each of the **verbs** in bold.

21 provide They bought the _provision_ at the supermarket.

22 enter They couldn't find the _entrance_ to the caves.

23 choose They had the _choice_ of going to the seaside or to a farm.

24 advertise The _Advertisment_ said that the concert started at 7.30 p.m.

25 perform The _performance_ of the school play was excellent.

26 bewilder The child's _bewilderness_ was plain to see.

27 destroy The army was responsible for the _Destroyed_ of the bridge.

28 applaud The _Applause_ was deafening.

~~7~~ 8

E 2

Fill in the missing letter in each word with an *a, e* or *o*.

29 decorat_o_r ✓   **30** cell_a_r ✓   **31** plumb_e_r ✓

32 disast_a_r ✗   **33** corrid_o_r ✓   **34** burgl_a_r ✓

35 popul_a_r ✓   **36** circul_a_r ✓   **37** divis_e_r ✗

38 direct_o_r ✓   **39** propriet_o_r ✓   **40** partn_e_r ✓

O 12

D 12

Write the following using indirect speech.

41–45 Dad said, "I am going to mow the lawn. I hope this is the last time I will have to do it this year as I am tired of doing it."

Dad said that _he is_ (was) going to mow the lawn. _(would)_

he hopes (would be) this _is_ ~~the last~~ the last time _he will_ (would)

have to do it this year as _he is_ (was) tired of doing it.

~~5~~

5

Write *there*, *their* or *they're* in each gap.

46–47 ~~their~~ they're going to dive into the pool when *their* teacher blows the whistle.

48–49 Where are ~~their~~ *their* coats? ~~there~~ *they're* soaking!

50–51 *there* is no point hiding the chocolate box *there*!

52–53 *there* is a strong wind which has blown some tiles off *their* roof.

Write the **contraction** for each of these.

54 they have _____ they've _____   55 I would _____ I'd _____

56 will not _____ won't _____

In each space, write the word class of the underlined word.

57 Close the <u>back</u> door.   behind adjective

58 We said we would <u>back</u> Hotspot to win the race.   support verb

59 Dad's got a pain in his <u>back</u>.   bone noun

60 Come <u>back</u> soon.   here adverb

Write three **compound words** using each of the words listed.

61–63 light   lighthouse _____ _____

64–66 snow   snowball   snowman   snowfight

67–69 day   day-glow _____ _____

Underline the unstressed vowels in each word.

70 postage   71 sentence   72 parliament

73 machinery   74 fattening   75 mathematics

76 history

Rewrite these **sentences** changing them from **singular** to **plural**.

77–80 The man was cleaning his house.

The men were cleaning ~~there~~ *their* houses

81–82 She jumped over the puddle.

they jumped ~~oot~~ over the Puddles ✓ +2

83–86 He bought a scarf to support his football team.

They bought some scarts to Support their football team 8 10

scarves

Underline the correct **homophone** in each sentence. E 2

87 The (principle/principal) message of the speech was that we all need to work together.

88 The midfielder (past, passed) the ball to the striker, who scored a goal.

89 We (rode, rowed) our bikes along the canal path until it became dark.

90 Do you know (who's, whose) car is blocking the drive?

91 My parents insist that we recycle whatever we can because they hate to (waste, waist) anything.

92 We followed the signs for the holiday (root, route) along the motorway.

93 I always turn away when I'm watching a nature programme that shows a lion catching its (prey, pray).

94 'Hurry or we are going (to, too) be late!'

95 The training (coarse, course) began at 9:00 in the morning. 7 9

Rewrite the passage adding the missing commas. D 4

96–100 Sam was caught thank goodness otherwise I would have been blamed for stealing the sweets pen magazine Harry Potter book and racing car.

Sam was caught, thank goodness, otherwise I would have been blamed for stealing the sweets, pen, magazine, Harry Potter book and racing car 4 5

It wasn't long before Jonathan Gull was off by himself again, far out to sea, hungry, happy, learning.

The subject was speed, and in a week's practice he learned more about speed than the fastest gull alive.

From a thousand feet, flapping his wings as hard as he could, he pushed over into a blazing steep dive towards the waves, and learned why seagulls don't make blazing steep power-dives. In just six seconds he was moving seventy miles per hour, the speed at which one's wing goes unstable on the upstroke.

Time after time it happened. Careful as he was, working at the very peak of his ability, he lost control at high speed.

Climb to a thousand feet. Full power straight ahead first, then push over, flapping, to a vertical dive. Then, every time, his left wing stalled on an upstroke, he'd roll violently left, stall his right wing recovering, and flick like fire into a wild tumbling spin to the right.

He couldn't be careful enough on that upstroke. Ten times he tried, and all ten times, as he passed through seventy miles per hour, he burst into a churning mass of feathers, out of control, crashing down into the water.

The key, he thought at last, dripping wet, must be to hold the wings still at high speeds – to flap up to fifty and then hold the wings still.

From two thousand feet he tried again, rolling into his dive, beak straight down, wings full out and stable from the moment he passed fifty miles per hour. It took tremendous strength, but it worked. In ten seconds he had blurred through ninety miles per hour. Jonathan had set a world speed record for seagulls!

But victory was short-lived. The instant he began his pullout, the instant he changed the angle of his wings, he snapped into the same terrible uncontrolled disaster, and at ninety miles per hour it hit him like dynamite. Jonathan Seagull exploded in midair and smashed down into a brick-hard sea.

When he came to, it was well after dark, and he floated in moonlight on the surface of the ocean. His wings were ragged bars of lead, but the weight of failure was even heavier on his back. He wished, feebly, that the weight could be just enough to drag him gently down to the bottom, and end it all.

As he sank low in the water, a strange hollow voice sounded within him. There's no way around it. I am a seagull. I am limited by my nature. If I were meant to learn so much about flying, I'd have charts for brains. If I were meant to fly at speed, I'd have a falcon's short wings, and live on mice instead of fish. My father was right. I must forget this foolishness. I must fly home to the Flock and be content as I am, as a poor limited seagull.

The voice faded, and Jonathan agreed. The place for a seagull at night is on shore, and from this moment forth, he vowed, he would be a normal gull. It would make everyone happier.

He pushed wearily away from the dark water and flew towards the land, grateful for what he had learned about work-saving low-altitude flying.

But no, he thought. I am done with the way I was, I am done with everything I learned. I am a seagull like every other seagull, and I will fly like one. So he climbed painfully to a hundred feet and flapped his wings harder, pressing for shore.

He felt better for his decision to be just another one of the flock. There would be no ties now to the force that had driven him to learn, there would be no more challenge and no more failure. And it was pretty, just to stop thinking, and fly through the dark, toward the lights above the beach.

Dark! The hollow voice cracked in alarm. *Seagulls never fly in the dark!*   50

Jonathan was not alert to listen. It's pretty, he thought. The moon and the lights twinkling on the water, throwing out little beacon-trails through the night, and all so peaceful and still … .

Get down! Seagulls never fly in the dark! If you were meant to fly in the dark, you'd have the eyes of an owl! You'd have charts for brains! You'd have a falcon's   55
short wings!

There in the night, a hundred feet in the air, Jonathan Livingston Seagull blinked. His pain, his resolutions, vanished.

Short wings. *A falcon's short wings!*

That's the answer! What a fool I've been! All I need is a tiny little wing, all I need   60
is to fold most of my wings and fly on just the tips alone! *Short wings!*

He climbed two thousand feet above the black sea, and without a moment for thought of failure and death, he brought his forewings tightly in to his body, left only the narrow swept daggers of his wingtips extended into the wind, and fell into a vertical dive.   65

The wind was a monster roar at his head. Seventy miles per hour, ninety, a hundred and twenty and faster still. The wing-strain now at a hundred and forty miles per hour wasn't nearly as hard as it had been before at seventy, and with the faintest twist of his wingtips he eased out of the dive and shot above the waves, a grey cannonball under the moon.   70

He closed his eyes to slits against the wind and rejoiced. A hundred and forty miles per hour! And under control! If I dive from five thousand feet instead of two thousand, I wonder how fast ..?

His vows of a moment before were forgotten, swept away in that great swift wind. Yet he felt guiltless, breaking the promises he had made himself. Such promises are   75
only for the gulls that accept the ordinary. One who has touched excellence in his learning has no need of that kind of promise.

From *Jonathan Livingston Seagull: A Story* by Richard Bach

Answer these questions.

1 At what speed did Jonathan stall each time?

seventy miles per hour ✓

2 Which wing caused Jonathan to stall?

his left wing ✓

3 From what height did Jonathan first break the world speed record for seagulls?

two thousand feet ✓

4 Write a **synonym** for the word 'tremendous' (line 22). brilliant huge ✓

5 What hit Jonathan like 'dynamite' (line 26)? ✗

The spin

6 Why, on line 27, was the sea described as 'brick-hard'? ✗

because he was so high up

7–8 Find two pieces of evidence in the passage that show how desperate Jonathan felt having crashed at ninety miles per hour. ✓

he wished that the weight on his back would sink. In to the bottom he talks to himself and says he will be a n gul

9 What does 'from this moment forth' (line 39) mean?

From know on ✓

10 Which bird is mentioned in the passage as having short wings? __Falcon__ ✓

11 Which **phrase** conveys Jonathan's true feelings about being a gull?

as a poor limited seagull ✓

12–13 Why was Jonathan 'not alert to listen' on line 51? Use evidence from the passage to support your answer.

because he says "It's pretty" and he kind of does not want to be a seagull ✗

14 Give one reason why gulls never fly in the dark.

Their wings are to long, ✗

15 Why did Jonathan blink in line 58? ✓

because he had found the answer

16–17 Jonathan is described as 'a grey cannonball' on line 70. Explain why this **phrase** is used.

because of the shadow under the moon $\frac{1}{2}$

18–20 Look at the final paragraph again. Describe the key characteristics of Jonathan Livingston Seagull. ✗

he is an extraordinary gull who does not want to be a gull.

$10\frac{1}{2}$ 20

10

Give the **plurals** of the following **nouns**.

21 mouse _mice_ ✓   22 story _Stories_ ✓

23 cargo/cargoes _Cargoes_ ✓   24 thief _thieves_ ✓

25 trolley _trolleys_ ✓   26 potato _potatoes_

27 gas _gases_ ✓   28 ox _oxen_ ✓

29 roof _rooves_ ✗   30 valley _valleys_ ✓
roofs

Match the words with their **definitions**. Write the correct number in the space.

31 conservation _2_   (1) secret ✗

32 constellation _4_   (2) assembly ✓

33 conversation _3_   (3) informal discussion ✓

34 confidential _1_   (4) group of stars ✓

35 consecutive _5_   (5) one after the other, in order ✓

36 congregation _6_   (6) preservation ✗

Put the words in bold in their correct places so the extract below makes sense.

37–46 **movement**   **wedge**   **cook**   **ashore**   **crutch**

deck   **walk**   **spaces**   **lanyard**   **heaviest**

✓ Long John Silver, our ship's _cook_ – Barbecue as the men called him –

carried his _crutch_ by a _movement_ ✗ round his neck, to have both hands as

free as possible. It was something to see him _wedge_ the foot of his

crutch against a bulkhead, and, propped against it, yielding to every

✗ _deck_ of the ship, get on with his cooking like someone safe _ashore_.

Still more strange was it to see him in the _heaviest_ of weather, cross the

✗ _lanyard_. He had a line or two rigged up to help him across the widest

spaces and he would hand himself from one place to another as quickly

as another man could _walk_. ✓

From *Treasure Island* by R L Stevenson

D 6

9 10

E 2

4 6

7 10

11

Complete the following **similes** using the words in the box.

two peas	pie	hatter	cucumber
lead	bat	cricket	gold

47 as alike as ___two peas___ ✓   48 as blind as a ___bat___ ✓

49 as cool as a ___cucumber___ ✗   50 as easy as ___pie___ ✓

51 as good as ___gold___ ✓   52 as heavy as ___lead___ ✓

53 as lively as a ___cricket___ ✓   54 as mad as a ___hatter___ ✓

Underline the **verbs** in the **sentences**.

55 Ian had a large appetite. ✗

56 Rachel wrote the invitations to her party neatly. ✓

57 She intently watched the TV programme. ✓

58 Softly she sang the lilting tune. ✓

59 They got up early on Sunday. ✓

60–61 He lifted the kitten carefully and put it in the basket. ½

Write an **antonym** for each of these words.

62 contract ___extract___ ✗   63 import ___deport___ ✗

64 increase ___decrease___ ✓   65 fine ___coarse/fine?___ ✓

66 captive ___free___   67 temporary ___permanent___

68 superior ___loser___ ✗   69 refuse ___accept___

70 plural ___singular___ ✓   71 destroy ___create___

Fill the gap by writing the **past tense** of the word in bold.

72 **creep**   They ___crept___ slowly towards her. ✓

73 **lose**   He ___lost___ his ball when he was out in the woods.

74 **speak**   The lady ___spoke___ kindly to the little girl. ✓

75 **ring**   The policewoman ___rang___ the doorbell. ✓

76 **break**   Mum was cross when they ___broke___ the plate. ✓

Circle the **pronouns** in the short passage.

77–83 They jumped into the car before it sped off at high speed. Joseph whispered that his mum had never been so cross. She reminded him of a bull! They agreed with him.

Copy and add the missing punctuation to the following:

84–88 What about the horse You don't mention sending that back said Thorin

"What about the horse? You don't mention sending that back," said Thorin.

Write three words using each of the **prefixes**.

89–91 **dis-** dismay disappoint disport

92–94 **mis-** missing miss misused

Identify what part of speech each of the words in bold are.

The **terrified people reacted badly** when they **were** asked to go in **another** direction.

95 verb 96 noun 97 verb

98 noun Adjective 99 pronoun 100 pronoun

adverb

Now go to the Progress Chart to record your score! Total 62 100

13

Snake

A snake came to my water-trough
On a hot, hot day, and I in pyjamas for the heat,
To drink there.

In the deep, strange-scented shade of the great dark carob-tree
I came down the steps with my pitcher   5
And must wait, must stand and wait, for there he was at the trough before me.

He reached down from a fissure in the earth-wall in the gloom
And trailed his yellow-brown slackness soft-bellied down, over the edge of the stone trough
And rested his throat upon the stone bottom,
And where the water had dripped from the tap, in a small clearness,   10
He sipped with his straight mouth,
Softly drank through his straight gums, into his slack long body,
Silently.

Someone was before me at my water-trough,
And I, like a second comer, waiting.   15

He lifted his head from his drinking, as cattle do,
And looked at me vaguely, as drinking cattle do,

And flickered his two-forked tongue from his lips, and mused a moment,
And stooped and drank a little more,
Being earth-brown, earth-golden from the burning bowels of the earth   20
On the day of Sicilian July, with Etna smoking.

The voice of my education said to me
He must be killed,
For in Sicily the black, black snakes are innocent, the gold are venomous.

And voices in me said, *If you were a man*   25
You would take a stick and break him now, and finish him off.

But must I confess how I liked him,
How glad I was he had come like a guest in quiet, to drink at my water-trough
And depart peaceful, pacified, and thankless,
Into the burning bowels of this earth?   30

Was it cowardice, that I dared not kill him?
Was it perversity, that I longed to talk to him?
Was it humility, to feel so honoured?
I felt so honoured.

And yet those voices: 35
If you were not afraid, you would kill him!

And truly I was afraid, I was most afraid,
But even so, honoured still more
That he should seek my hospitality
From out the dark door of the secret earth.   40

He drank enough
And lifted his head, dreamily, as one who has drunken,
And flickered his tongue like a forked night on the air, so black,
Seeming to lick his lips,
And looked around like a god, unseeing, into the air,   45
And slowly turned his head.

And slowly, very slowly, as if thrice adream,
Proceeded to draw his slow length curving round
And climb again the broken bank of my wall-face …

… I looked round, I put down my pitcher,   50
I picked up a clumsy log
And threw it at the water-trough with a clatter.

I think it did not hit him,
But suddenly that part of him that was left behind convulsed in undignified haste,
Writhing like lightning, and was gone   55
Into the black hole, the earth-lipped fissure in the wall-front,
At which, in the intense still noon, I stared with fascination.

And immediately I regretted it.
I thought how paltry, how vulgar, what a mean act!

I despised myself and the voices of my accursed human education.   60
And I thought of the albatross,
And I wished he would come back, my snake …

by D H Lawrence

Answer these questions.

1 What was at the water-trough when the writer arrived? A snake ✓

2 Which **adjective** does the poet use to describe the snake's mouth?
Straight ✓

3 In lines 16–17 the snake was compared to cattle. How?   × ½
by lifting his head up like cattle do.
and by look looking vaguely as drinking cattle do

4 Did this scene take place during the day or at night?
The day, it says so in line 2 ✓

15

5–7 Give the meaning of the following words as they are used in the poem:

'mused' (line 18) _paused_ x _pondered._

'venomous' (line 24) _poisonous_ ✓

'perversity' (line 32) _curiosity Curiosity_ x

8 Copy a line from the poem that indicates in which country the scene is based.

For in Sicily the black, black snakes are innocent ✓ _renown_

9 Find a line or **phrase** that is characteristically used to describe a snake.

Softly drank through his straight gums into his x _long body_

10 Line 34 reads 'I felt so honoured'. Why did the onlooker feel like this?

because the snake is rare x

11 Why does the poet describe the earth as 'secret' (line 40)?

because the snake does not know about earth. x

12–13 Look again at lines 31–40. Using lines from the poem to support your answer, describe how the onlooker is feeling.

The onlooker is honoured as it says ½ _Humility to feel so honoured he is also afraid._

14–15 What is the snake's attitude while at the drinking trough? Use a line from the poem to support your answer.

he was very calm and very silent as it says silently x

16 The onlooker picked up 'a clumsy log' (line 51). Why was the log described as 'clumsy'?

because he picked it up in a clumsy way x

17 Using evidence from the poem, explain why the onlooker threw a log at the snake.

So he would move from the trough and he could drink x

18–19 Describe the physical environment of where the poem is taking place. Use an example from the passage to support your answer.

"Where etna etna was. Smoking"
"It was also a hot hot day".

20 What is the main point made in the final verse of the poem? *an out of time!*

Underline the words below which are of common gender.

21–27

actress	athlete	student	widow
policeman	friend	dustman	typist
knitter	bride	bachelor	mother
girl	child	cat	businessman

Write the following **abbreviations** in full.

28 NE _____

29 PLC _____

30 PTO _____

31 Dept _____

32 mg _____

33 BST _____

34 UK _____

Complete each expression with a **preposition**.

Example *off* the cuff

35 _____ the most part

36 _____ the long run

37 _____ all fours

38 _____ the other hand

39 _____ better or worse

40 _____ his wits' end

41 _____ all means

42 _____ to the hilt

Complete the following words with *ie* or *ei*.

43 for____gn   44 bel____ve   45 ach____ve

46 conc____ted   47 n____ghbour   48 aud____nce

49 h____ght   50 c____ling

E 2

8

D 6

On each line, underline the word which is the same part of speech as the word in bold.

51 **often**	noble	beautiful	sick	badly	wanting
52 **breathe**	quickly	goat	it	for	slither
53 **height**	quantity	sit	idle	lazy	comfortable
54 **difficult**	soften	woollen	they	worm	grew
55 **why**	time	place	where	town	hour
56 **sad**	dress	bonnet	ship	picture	ugly
57 **and**	sand	boat	badly	but	cut

7

E 2

Write two words that use the **root word** in bold.

58–59 **help**   _____   _____

60–61 **turn**   _____   _____

62–63 **collect**   _____   _____

64–65 **reason**   _____   _____

66–67 **agree**   _____   _____

10

D 6

Underline any of these words which should always start with a capital letter.

68–76   envelope   egyptian   film   david   february

wales   food   function   denmark   nation

month   june   manchester   ornament   tuesday

queen   kite   britney   log   lion

9

E 2

Spell these words correctly.

77 Febuary   _____

78 tomorow   _____

79 posess   _____

80 goverment   _____

4

Make **nouns** from the words in bold to complete the **sentences**.

D 6

81 punish   I do not believe in capital _____.

82 fragrant   The _____ of the rose was beautiful.

83 arrive   The _____ of the pop star at the airport was delayed.

84 long   Sarah said that her trousers were not the right _____.

85 conclude   At the _____ of the concert we rushed to get home.

86 assist   Dad asked Najib for his _____.

6

D 13

Rewrite these **sentences** so they contain only single negatives.

87 Gina didn't swim in no sea.

_____

88 There weren't no stars out tonight.

_____

89 The dogs didn't not wait.

_____

90 The playground wasn't not open.

_____

91 Caroline didn't want no ride in the car.

_____

92 Raj's family hadn't won no money on the lottery.

_____

6

D 5

Write eight **contractions** using the words in bold.

are	**you**	**have**	**will**	**they**	**not**

93–100 _____   _____   _____   _____

        _____   _____   _____   _____

8

Why grow vegetables?

What can I say to the enthusiastic cook who is vaguely interested in the idea of growing his or her own vegetables but is still teetering on the brink of action? Realistically, for most of us these days there are no persuasive economic arguments for growing your own vegetables – at least, not if you cost out your time. (During 5
summer gluts, my father used to pay me pocket money to pick and freeze peas, beans and soft fruits from his vegetable garden. He once calculated that the resulting frozen produce cost him three or four times what it would in the supermarket. And that was without factoring in his own time.)

But there is still an important sense in which the vegetables you grow yourself 10
really are free. When your time is given freely, what you make with it is free in the best sense of the word. When you buy your vegetables, you are a slave – to the car that takes you to the shops; to the methods, good and bad, by which the vegetables are produced; to the market forces, and the big bosses who fix the prices; to the shelf-stacking policies that determine the freshness, or otherwise, of 15
the produce you buy. You have no say whatsoever in the means of production, no role in the quality of what becomes yours only when you hand over the cash.

Grow your own vegetables and all that changes. Choose the seeds, the growing site, the time to plant, to weed, to water, to feed, to harvest. What you then take to the kitchen is not just a vegetable, it's a form of self-expression, an assertion of 20
personal liberty. It's a kind of opting out of the world as you're told it must be in favour of the world as you'd like it to be. You may doubt the wisdom of loading something as ordinary as a carrot with such deep personal meaning. But try growing them yourself, and you will find that carrots are far from ordinary. They are sleek, pointed, orange miracles that come from nowhere to populate a bare patch 25
of earth. And, almost astonishingly, you can eat them!

The fact is, those who already grow their own vegetables for the kitchen need no converting to the cause. I have yet to meet a vegetable gardener who complained that 'it's hardly worth it, what with the choice available in the supermarket these

days', or 'it's too much time for too little reward', or 'what's the point, you can hardly   *30*
taste the difference anyway?' These quotations are the clichés of the uninitiated
– those who do not yet know the prickly heat of a fat radish freshly drawn from the
earth, washed with a quick wipe on a dewy tuft of grass, then eaten without further
ado; those who have not tasted the extra sugar dose in a pile of self-podded peas
thrown into boiling water within an hour of being picked; those who have not   *35*
marvelled at the unrepentant earthiness of freshly dug potatoes …

    If you are still wavering, let me offer you another, almost glib answer to the
question, 'why grow vegetables?' Because you can. I mean, anyone can. As I said
earlier, growing vegetables is easy. All you need is earth and seeds. Sunshine and
water are important too, but in a reasonable year both should come in plentiful   *40*
supply, courtesy of the man upstairs. A relaxed, *laissez-faire* attitude to growing
vegetables will stand the beginner in good stead. While there is plenty of scope
for fussing and fretting about your vegetable patch, you will probably find that
obsessional attention to detail either does or doesn't evolve as the years go by,
according to your personality. In other words, if you want to become the manic   *45*
overseer of a manicured vegetable plot, you can; but it doesn't have to start off
that way.

Starting a vegetable garden

Some thought is required in choosing your patch of ground. All gardeners have to
compromise, and while a south-facing, level piece of land, sheltered from the worst   *50*
of the wind, with a rich, finely textured soil will get you off to a flying start, few of us
are blessed with such perfect growing conditions. It's more a question of avoiding
negative factors. Light is vital, and a patch that is in near-permanent shade is simply
not going to work. It's important, therefore, to be aware of the passage of the sun
across your intended growing site from dawn till dusk. If the ground enjoys direct   *55*
sunlight for more than half of daylight hours (that's about four in mid-winter, eight
on the longest day), you should be able to grow well on it. It's worth bearing in
mind that you may be able to gain extra sunlight for your patch by cutting down an
unfortunately located tree or two. This takes a bit of courage, and there's no point in
breaking your heart by sacrificing a beloved feature of your garden for an extra row   *60*
of peas. But trees are not sacred just because they are big. And of course there's
the firewood bonus.

    As far as the timing of your bed-creation scheme goes, you have two choices:
late autumn for planting the following spring, or early spring for almost immediate
planting. An autumn digging will give the soil a chance to settle and leaves time   *65*
for existing green matter, such as grass tufts and the usual weeds, to rot down.
The winter months ahead will allow this to happen without too many new weeds
springing up. However, you will have to be on your toes come spring, as the weed
seeds in the ground will leap at the first chance they get to germinate and take
hold. Another good going over in early March will be essential if you don't want to   *70*
be back to square one. If you're opting for spring digging, you may as well wait
until it's almost time to start planting: say early April. Dig over your patch, removing
all the grass and weeds you can, and simply work over your soil till it is nicely
broken up and ready for planting.

From *The River Cottage Cookbook* by Hugh Fearnley-Whittingstall

Answer these questions.

1 What did the author's father used to pay him to do?

_____

2 What is meant by 'teetering on the brink of action' (line 3)?

_____

3–5 List and explain three reasons why the author suggests it is not good to buy vegetables.

_____

_____

_____

6 Which vegetable does the author use to inspire vegetable growers?

_____

7 Who needs no converting to the vegetable-growing cause?

_____

8 Does the author believe growing vegetables is easy or hard? _____

9–11 Which four key things do you need to grow vegetables? Explain why.

_____

_____

_____

_____

12 Describe what is meant by a 'laissez-faire attitude' on line 41.

_____

13 What is the meaning of the word 'compromise' (line 50) in this context?

_____

14 Why has the author described the trees as 'unfortunately located' (line 59)?

_____

_____

_____

15–17 Find three examples from the passage conveying the author's passion for growing vegetables.

_____

_____

_____

18–20 The next subtitle in the author's book is 'Preparing for sowing'. Write three things the author might cover under this heading.

_____

_____

_____

Write three **onomatopoeic** words that describe sounds made by the following:

21–23 an engine   _____   _____   _____

24–26 the wind   _____   _____   _____

27–29 water   _____   _____   _____

Add a different **suffix** to each of these **root words**. Rewrite the words correctly.

30 swim   _____   **31** experiment _____

32 use   _____   **33** excite   _____

34 thought   _____   **35** child   _____

36 marry   _____   **37** excel   _____

38 bore   _____

Rewrite the **phrases** below in more formal English.

39 See ya later.

_____

40 You're taking the mickey!

_____

41 Did you wag school?

_____

42 It was an awesome gig.

_____

43 You look cool in those sunglasses.

_____ ⬤ 5

D 5

Add the missing colons.

44 The following children are absent today Amina, Ilesh, Frank, Michael and Fayza.

45 The school magazine reported No school uniform for a day!

46 An eyewitness stated The car turned over as it crashed into the tree, just missing three people ...

47 The following classes are out on a school trip today Class 6L, Class 6T and Class 6M.

48 The local paper reported School flooded, children sent home. ⬤ 5

E 2

The following words end in either _ent_ or _ant_. Add the correct ending to each word.

49 eleg_____   **50** prud_____   **51** adjac_____

52 abund_____   **53** arrog_____   **54** extravag_____

55 contin_____   **56** immigr_____   **57** cem_____ ⬤ 9

D 8

Circle the **diminutives**.

58–64
golden	gosling	classroom	penknife
statuette	droplet	daylight	hamlet
duckling	starlet	appearance	majorette

⬤ 7

D 6

Write the possessive form of each of the following.

65 food for the rabbit   _____

66 hairbrush for Leanne   _____

67 football for the players   _____

68 café for the museum   _____

69 handlebar of a bicycle   _____

70 newspaper for Mr Dodd   _____

6

E 2

Improve these **sentences** by changing the group of words in bold for a single one.

71 The children were delighted to be able to talk to the **person who wrote the**

book. _____

72 The teacher put the **pens, rulers, pencils and rubbers** in the cupboard.

_____

73 Peter **said he was sorry** for what he had done. _____

74 The weather has improved **during the last day or two**. _____

75 The children who were **at school that day** put up the decorations.

_____

76 Gareth thought it **a waste of time** to copy the words of the song when he could already sing it perfectly.

_____

6

E 2

Write words with the following number of syllables.

   77 2 syllables   _____

78–79 3 syllables   _____   _____

80–81 4 syllables   _____   _____

82–83 5 syllables   _____   _____

84–85 6 syllables   _____   _____

9

Rewrite the passage, adding the missing punctuation. Start new lines where necessary.

86–100 I will buy you some new shoes said Mum but not until you have out-grown the ones you are wearing now But these aren't fashionable complained Sam Nobody has shoes like these now Mum just laughed

_____

_____

_____

_____

_____

15

Now go to the Progress Chart to record your score! **Total** 100

Paper 5

B

The Adventures of Huckleberry Finn *was written by Mark Twain. His real name was Samuel Clemens but he chose the name 'Mark Twain' while working as a Mississippi river pilot. It was a term used for a water depth of 2 fathoms at which it was considered safe to sail along. After working on the river he then became a reporter, until finally spending his time as an author. He lived from 1835 to 1910.*

The character Huckleberry Finn was one of an outcast. He was abandoned by his father at a young age. He never wished for a 'normal' life of going to school and having home-comforts around; instead, he liked the freedom to spend his days however he wanted, living close to nature. This produced many an adventure!

We judged that three more nights would fetch us to Cairo, at the bottom of Illinois, where the Ohio River comes in, and that was what we was after. We would sell the raft and get on a steamboat and go way up the Ohio amongst the free States, and then be out of trouble.

Well, the second night a fog begun to come on, and we made for a tow-head to   5
tie to, for it wouldn't do to try to run in fog; but when I paddled ahead in the canoe, with the line, to make fast, there warn't anything but little saplings to tie to. I passed the line around one of them right on the edge of the cut bank, but there was a stiff current, and the raft come booming down so lively she tore it out by but the roots and away she went. I see the fog closing down, and it made me so sick and scared   10
I couldn't budge for most a half a minute it seemed to me – and then there warn't no raft in sight; you couldn't see twenty yards. I jumped into the canoe and run back to the stern and grabbed the paddle and set her back a stroke. But she didn't come. I was in such a hurry I hadn't untied her. I got up and tried to untie her, but I was so excited my hands shook so I couldn't hardly do anything with them.   15

As soon as I got started I took out after the raft, hot and heavy, right down the tow-head. That was all right as far as it went, but the tow-head warn't sixty yards long, and the minute I flew by the foot of it I shot out into the solid white fog, and hadn't no more idea which way I was going than a dead man.

Thinks I, it won't do to paddle; first I know I'll run into the bank or a tow-head or   20
something; I got to set still and float, and yet it's mighty fidgety business to have to hold your hands still at such a time. I whooped and listened. Away down there, somewheres, I hear a small whoop, and up comes my spirits. I went tearing after it, listening sharp to hear it again. The next time it come, I see I warn't heading for it but heading away to the right of it. And the next time, I was heading away to the left   25
of it – and not gaining on it much, either, for I was flying around, this way and that and t'other, but it was going straight ahead all the time.

I did wish the fool would think to beat a tin pan, and beat it all the time, but he never did, and it was the still places between the whoops that was making the trouble for me. Well, I fought along, and directly I hears the whoop *behind* me. I was   30
tangled good, now. That was somebody else's whoop, or else I was turned around.

I throwed the paddle down. I heard the whoop again; it was behind me yet, but in a different place; it kept coming, and kept changing its place, and I kept answering, till by-and-by it was in front of me again and I knowed the current had swung the canoe's head down-stream and I was all right, if that was Jim and not some other   35
raftsman hollering. I couldn't tell nothing about voices in a fog, for nothing don't look natural nor sound natural in a fog.

From *The Adventures of Huckleberry Finn* by Mark Twain

Answer these questions.

1 Where did Mark Twain get the idea for his name?

_____

2 Huckleberry Finn was an 'outcast'. Describe what is meant by 'outcast'.

_____

3 Where was Huckleberry Finn heading? _____

4 With whom was Huckleberry Finn travelling? _____

5 On which night did the fog descend? _____

6 The river current is described as 'stiff' (line 8). Which event in the passage illustrates this?

_____

7–8 Find two pieces of evidence from the passage that help us appreciate how thick the fog was.

_____

_____

9–10 Huckleberry Finn felt 'scared' and 'excited' in this passage. Describe why you think he felt each of these emotions.

scared_____

excited_____

11 Why was Huckleberry Finn travelling at night?

_____

12 Find a word in the passage that means 'shouting' or 'shouted'. _____

13 What was Huckleberrry Finn frightened would happen as he untied the canoe and began to move?

_____

14–16 Which three things combined made Huckleberry Finn feel so lost in the canoe while trying to track the sound?

_____

_____

_____

17 Why do you think 'nothing don't look natural nor sound natural in a fog' (lines 36–37)?

_____

18–20 In your own words describe Huckleberry Finn's character. Use two pieces of evidence from the passage to support your answer.

_____

_____

_____ ◯ 20

[D 6]

To each **verb** add an **adverb** that could describe it.

21 spent _____ **22** ate _____

23 shone _____ **24** remembered _____

25 listened _____ **26** wrote _____

27 fought _____ **28** helped _____ ◯ 8

[E 2]

Complete each **sentence** with the correct **homophone**.

29–30 enquiry inquiry

The politician wanted an _____ into the way an _____ was made about his private life.

31–32 formally formerly

The headteacher _____ requested Mrs. Frampton, _____ a pupil of the school, to join the school governors.

33–34 beach beech

The _____ tree was in a garden quite near the _____. ◯ 6

[E 2]

Match these words with their meanings. Write the number of the correct **definition** by each word.

(1) a single rail track
(2) a series of sounds of the same pitch
(3) a single colour: black and white
(4) a word of one syllable
(5) design using initials of a name
(6) a speech performed by one actor
(7) one large block of stone

35 monochrome _____   **36** monogram _____

37 monolith _____   **38** monologue _____

39 monorail _____   **40** monosyllable _____

41 monotone _____

7

D 9
E 2

Add a **prefix** to make each of these words into its **antonym**.

42 lock _____   **43** polite _____

44 agree _____   **45** capable _____

46 regular _____   **47** own _____

48 reliable _____

7

E 2

Rewrite these sentences changing them from **plural** to **singular**.

49–51 The mice lived in the old barn until the children found them.

_____

52–54 The classes lined up quietly once their teachers had arrived.

_____

55–59 The satsumas were eaten quickly by the children, who then wanted some chocolates!

_____

_____

11

E 2

60–65 Put these words in reverse **alphabetical order**.

transfuse   transference   transfusion   transfer   transfigure   transformer

60 (1) _____   **61** (2) _____   **62** (3) _____

63 (4) _____   **64** (5) _____   **65** (6) _____

6

D 4
D 5

Rewrite the sentence and punctuate the passage correctly.

66–75 What time are you going home? said Jill to her brother I don't want to be late Tim replied Ill go when you are ready

_____

_____

_____

10

Add a **clause** to each of these to make a longer **sentence**. Use a different **connective** each time.

D 2

76–77 Zoe sprinted, just staying ahead _____

_____

78–79 Zoe sprinted, just staying ahead _____

_____

80–81 Zoe sprinted, just staying ahead _____

_____

82–83 Jack kept his eyes firmly on the ground _____

_____

84–85 Jack kept his eyes firmly on the ground _____

_____

86–87 Jack kept his eyes firmly on the ground _____

_____

12

Write these words in their **singular** form.

E 2

88 salmon _____

89 wives _____

90 opportunities _____

91 matrices _____

92 cacti _____

93 solos _____

94 appendices _____

95 puppies _____

8

Complete each **sentence** as a **metaphor**, using each **phrase** in the box once only.

C 4

| cotton wool | blanket | veil of darkness | shimmering river | soft cushion |

96 The _____ of snow lay on the fields.

97 The night was a _____.

98 The leaves were a _____ for the falling apples.

99 The _____ clouds hid the stars.

100 The wet road was a _____.

5

Now go to the Progress Chart to record your score! Total 100

The wind was a torrent of darkness among the gusty trees,
The moon was a ghostly galleon tossed upon cloudy seas,
The road was a ribbon of moonlight over the purple moor,
And the highwayman came riding –
    Riding – riding –   5
The highwayman came riding, up to the old inn-door.

He'd a French cocked-hat on his forehead, a bunch of lace at his chin,
A coat of claret velvet, and breeches of brown doe skin;
They fitted with never a wrinkle: his boots were up to the thigh!
And he rode with a jewelled tinkle,   10
    His pistol butts a-twinkle,
His rapier hilt a-twinkle, under the jewelled sky.

Over the cobbles he clattered and clashed in the dark inn-yard,
And he tapped with his whip on the shutters, but all was locked and barred;
He whistled a tune to the window, and who should be waiting there   15
But the landlord's black-eyed daughter,
    Bess, the landlord's daughter,
Plaiting a dark red love-knot into her long black hair.

And dark in the old inn-yard a stable-wicket creaked
Where Tim the ostler listened; his face was white and peaked;   20
His eyes were hollows of madness, his hair like mouldy hay,
But he loved the landlord's daughter,
    The landlord's red-lipped daughter;
Dumb as a dog he listened, and he heard the robber say –

'One kiss, my bonny sweetheart, I'm after a prize tonight,   25
But I shall be back with the yellow gold before the morning light;
Yet, if they press me sharply, and harry me through the day,
Then look for me by moonlight,
    Watch for me by moonlight,
I'll come to thee by moonlight, though hell should bar the way.'   30

He rose upright in the stirrups; he scarce could reach her hand,
But she loosened her hair i' the casement! His face burnt like a brand
As the black cascade of perfume came tumbling over his breast;
And he kissed its waves in the moonlight,
    (Oh, sweet black waves in the moonlight!)   35
Then he tugged at his rein in the moonlight, and galloped away to the west.

From *The Highwayman* by Alfred Noyes

Answer these questions.

1 At what time of day was this poem set? _____

2 What was 'a ribbon of moonlight'? _____

3 What colour was The Highwayman's coat? _____

4 How many people do we know were in love with the landlord's daughter?

_____

5 Explain what is meant by the words 'jewelled sky' (line 12).

_____

6–8 Highlight three distinct differences between The Highwayman and Tim.

_____

_____

_____

9 Why do you think Tim was described as 'Dumb as a dog' (line 24)?

_____

_____

10–11 What prize do you think The Highwayman was after? Which line in the passage conveys this?

_____

_____

12 Who might 'harry' (line 27) The Highwayman?

_____

13–15 How would you describe the landlord's daughter, as shown in the poem?

_____

_____

_____

16 The Highwayman is a narrative poem. What is a narrative poem?

_____

17–20 Explore the ways in which the poet creates the sense of confidence surrounding The Highwayman. Support your answer with lines from the poem.

_____

_____

Underline the word which is the same part of speech as the word in bold.

21 **laughed**   loudly   longer   ran   wild   joker

22 **magazine**   entered   cassette   he   wrote   her

23 **tiny**   bee   wasp   flew   away   large

24 **sang**   cried   loudly   nice   silently   nation

25 **loudly**   quickly   quieten   quicken   game   film

26 **they**   boys   children   she   teacher   class

Add the **suffix** *able* or *ful* to the words.

27 love _____   28 use _____   29 plenty _____

30 wonder _____   31 value _____   32 laugh _____

33 right _____   34 power _____   35 work _____

Some of the following pairs of words are **synonyms** and some are **antonyms**. Put them in the correct columns in the table.

36–45   vacant/empty   absence/presence   tranquil/peaceful

option/choice   seldom/often   few/many   here/there

caution/care   coarse/fine   famous/noted

Synonyms	Antonyms

Underline any word below which does not have a specifically feminine form.

    Example   actor ➝ actress   builder ➝ no specific feminine form

46–52   visitor   hero   waiter   worker

    manager   editor   relation   widower

    adult   mayor   pupil   passenger

Add the missing commas to these sentences.

53–54 One morning as the sun was rising Jack crept out of the house.

55 In his hand was a small bag just large enough to carry an apple two sandwiches and a big slice of cake.

56–57 He turned looked towards the house then ran across the field.

58 Jack moved slowly worried he might be seen.

59–61 As he entered the cave his eyes adjusting to the darkness he recognised the silhouette of Aimee his young and vulnerable sister.

Spell these words correctly.

62 buisness _____   **63** imaginry _____

64 consience _____   **65** enviroment _____

66 miscelaneous _____   **67** persasion _____

68 stomache _____   **69** necesary _____

70 possesion _____   **71** seqence _____

Copy and add the missing apostrophes.

72 five tigers tails _____

73 nine cows calves _____

74 three mens suits _____

75 four gates hinges _____

76 one dogs bone _____

Write the **abbreviation** of each of these.

77 centimetre _____   **78** kilogram _____

79 litre _____   **80** millimetre _____

81 square _____   **82** for example _____

83 number _____   **84** that is _____

Underline the **adjectival phrase** in each **sentence**.

85 I was pleased when the film, frightening and full of suspense, was over!

86 The morning snow, beautiful but cold, had settled outside my bedroom window.

87 The wild horse, dappled grey with a tangled mane, drank silently at the water's edge.

88 Last night's homework, confusing and difficult, took Nina many hours to complete.

89 Our local swimming pool, green, murky and a little smelly, hadn't been cleaned recently.

90 Ben, strong and athletic, was a capable athlete.

6

These are three ways in which words are derived. Write the appropriate number next to each word to show where you think it came from:

E 2

    (1) imitating a sound

    (2) another language

    (3) name of a place or person

91 moo   _____   92 cardigan   _____

93 autograph   _____   94 pizza   _____

95 biro   _____   96 whoosh   _____

6

Add the missing semicolons to these **sentences**.

D 5

97 Capital punishment no longer takes place in Great Britain it is still used in America.

98 Helen loves doing homework Laura prefers to socialise.

99 We visited the crown jewels jewels indeed fit for a queen.

100 An art gallery in London has a collection of Monet pictures an exhibition which is simply too good to miss.

4

Now go to the Progress Chart to record your score!   **Total**   100

A Dahl of a day out

For a whizzpopping day out, grab the kids and head for Great Missenden.

'It even smells like chocolate!' cries Dougie, aged 7, as we enter the Roald Dahl Museum and Story Centre in Great Missenden, Bucks. It looks like I'm onto a winner already. My challenge for the day is to help keep my nephew and his 9-year-old sister Meg entertained during the school holidays. So we've taken a short spin out of London – only 45 minutes or so – up the M40 to find out just how much fun   5
we can have in a museum dedicated to the greatest children's author of his generation.

According to Dahl's widow Liccy, there are four things her late husband really didn't like: beards, committees, speeches and museums. So don't attach too much significance to the word 'Museum' in the title of this place: Roald may not have approved of dusty, fusty edifices with squeaky glossed floors and highly polished   10
glass cabinets, but this hi-tech interactive playground for kids would surely have earned his approval.

As soon as we arrive, children are presented with a booklet entitled 'My Story Ideas'. It has a picture of Dahl scribbling away in his writer's hut on the cover, and as children wend their way round the small but well-designed museum, they are   15
encouraged to use it as a mini-scrapbook, filling it with stamps and pictures as they go round. 'I can finish this when I get home,' says Meg, clutching the book as we charge through the chocolate doors to the first gallery, titled Boy.

This room is the most traditional part of the museum, providing an insight into Dahl's childhood and a peek into his personal archive. There are letters sent home   20
from boarding school, reports ('very much improved' in English composition), and interactive touch-screen computer displays, cleverly designed to look like old school exercise books. These give adults a nostalgia trip while the kids press the screen and get the background info on their hero's work. I could have spent more time here, but the children have other ideas. 'The next room has puppets in it!' says   25
Dougie, who's been checking out what else lies in store.

Inside the Solo gallery, a giant video screen projects images from the movie version of *James and the Giant Peach* to a background of the title music from Dahl's hit TV series from the 1970s, *Tales of the Unexpected*. But, it's the *BFG*'s dream bottle in the centre of the room that has children flocking. Here they create their   30
own puppet shadow display. 'You can make your own show with a crocodile on a stick,' Dougie explains enthusiastically when I ask him what he likes most about this part. Meg meanwhile is investigating the stamps that print Quentin Blake's exquisite illustrations for Dahl's children's books onto card. 'It's a really good idea,' she says, proudly showing me *The Enormous Crocodile* she's just inked onto a postcard   35
that the museum conveniently provides for the kids. The carpet on the floor bears a single line from one of Dahl's notebooks in his barely legible script: 'Those who don't believe in magic will never find it.'

Before heading into the next gallery – the Story Centre of the title – we stop off for a comfort break. 'That gave me a fright', says Dougie, giggling madly as the loo   40 emits an alarming whizzpopping noise, replaced a minute later by the voice of the great man himself declaring, 'I will not eat worms!'

You can also investigate the inside of a faithful recreation of Dahl's beloved writing hut. Here we discovered some of the precious objects he kept on his desk including a huge ball of foil made up of chocolate bar wrappers that he'd eaten and a piece of his own hip bone removed during an operation ('Yuk!' exclaimed Meg gleefully). Everything is designed to be opened and closed, twiddled and fiddled, so that nosey, interfering children and their equally enquiring parents and guardians can enjoy the play value of the place without being told off – or getting dirty looks from the staff. 45 50

Our last stop is Miss Honey's Schoolroom where it is story time. A couple of energetic young guys acted out tales from Dahl's *Revolting Rhymes* with such infectious enthusiasm that I seriously feared for the health of one young man who puffs so much during *Tale of the Three Little Piggies* that he practically starts hyperventilating. The spellbound audience squeals delightedly as he goes redder and redder in the face. But his performance does not go unappreciated by the young audience. 'I thought you were just going to read to us,' says Dougie afterwards as he chats happily to the reader, 'but you acted out the stories too, and that was really funny.' 55

Article by Damien Kelleher

Answer these questions.

1 In which county is the museum? _Bucks (Buckinghamshire)_ ✓

2 Who is Liccy? _Liccy's Dahl's Widow_ ✓

3–4 Find two pieces of evidence in the passage of the museum's links with Dahl's book *Charlie and the Chocolate Factory*.
The chocolate doors and the Chocolate bar wrappers. ✓

5 Why is the museum described as a 'hi-tech interactive playground for kids'?
It's a Modern, uptodate museum that allows children to...

6 In which gallery were Dahl's letters and school reports?
They are in the gallery named boy ✓

7 Why would interactive displays of old school exercise books give adults a 'nostalgia trip'?
Because the old school exercise books probably... ✓

8 When did Roald Dahl have a hit TV series? _1970's_ ✓

9 Explain in your own words what Dahl meant by 'Those who don't believe in magic will never find it' (lines 37–38).

Dahl Means that if you open your Mind and think about being in a diffent world you will enjoy it or not!!

10–11 What is a 'comfort break' (line 40) and how is the experience different?

A comfort break is a Loo. The experience is different because it is a Roald Dahl Loo with sound effects

12 Why is Roald Dahl described as 'the great man' (line 42)?

Because he is the greatest childrens writer!

13 What is the meaning of the word 'edifices' on line 10?

Houses of some sort x buildings

14–16 Give three reasons why Roald Dahl would approve of this museum. Use evidence from the article to support your answer.

Because the children are allowed to touch everything (This hitech interactive playground would surely earn his approval)

17–18 Describe the sort of person Roald Dahl is, as shown in this article.

I think he is a very good children's author. I also think he sounds quite fun and kind.

19–20 Who is the intended audience for this article? Explain your answer.

People who want to take there their children to fun places.

Fill the gap by writing the past tense of the word in bold.

21 run The children ___ran___ as fast as they could in the race. ✓

22 try I wasn't pleased with my score, but I had ___tried___ my best. ✓

23 sleep The noise of the plane meant that I only ___slept___ for a few hours. ✓

24 feel I ___felt___ pleased when I was told that Emma was coming to visit.

25 see When we ___saw___ the presents we were very excited.

26 find Luckily, Jamal ___found___ his wallet and keys. ✓

27 meet We __Met__ last Wednesday after lunch. ✓

28 build The new house on our block was __built__ in less than six months. ✓

29 begin The concert __began__ on time. ✓

9 | 9

D | 5

Write the possessive form of each of these **phrases**, i.e. with an apostrophe.

Example The funnels of the ships   The ships' funnels

30 The cars of the teachers   The teachers' cars ✓

31 The cat of my cousin   My cousin's Cat ✓

32 The umbrellas of the children   The children's umbrellas ✓

33 The bank account of the woman   The woman's ~~of the~~ bank account ✓

34 The guitars of the singers   The singers' guitars ✓

35 The chair of the dentist   The dentist's chair ✓

36 The walls of the flats   The flats' walls ✓

7 | 7

C | 4

Write two **onomatopoeic** words for each of these subjects.

37–38 water   Splash ✓   ✗

39–40 a volcano   Bang ~~✗~~   Crash ✓

41–42 a tree   ✗   ✗

2 | 6

D | 6

Complete the following **sentences** by writing a different **preposition** in each space.

43 He climbed __up__ the gate with ease. ✓

44 Mark corresponds __with__ two penfriends. ✓

45 Granny is suffering __From__ arthritis.

46 We walked slowly __to__ the river bank. ✓

47 Her paper was hidden __under__ the pile of books. ✓

48 Keep your head __above__ the water when learning to swim. ✓

49 I put it __in__ the radiator. ✗

50 We waited __on__ the bus. ✓

7 | 8

40

Write the root of each of the words.

51 significant _____ ✗   **52** happiness _____ *happy* ✓

53 dutiful _____ *duty* ✓   **54** prestigious _____ ✗

55 heavily _____ *heavy* ✓   **56** predate _____ ✗

57 independent _____ ✗   **58** confession _____ *Confess* ✓

④ 8

In the following passage there are blanks. The jumbled word in brackets, when the letters are rearranged, makes a word to fill the blank.

59–69 Last _____ *Saturday* ✓ **(aaurStdy)** my friend and I went to a Dog Show.

First we saw the _____ ✗ **(Obcdeeein)** Class. The dogs had to

_____ ✗ **(narmei)** where they were, even though their _____ *owners* ✓

(swoner) had walked away. There were _____ *several* **(verseal)** other

classes. One was for _____ *toy* ✓ **(oyt)** dogs, another was for

_____ ✗ **(trrreeis)** and a third was for _____ ✗ **(hsunod)**. The

_____ *Judge* **(jusdeg)** looked carefully at the _____ ✗ **(slamina)** before

awarding the _____ *prize* ✓ **(pzesir)**.

⑥ 11

Underline the correct word in the brackets.

70 Not one of the children (<u>are</u>, is) allowed in the sea. ✗

71 All of you but one (<u>have</u>, has) brothers ✓

72 Neither of the children (<u>are</u>, is) from this town. ✗

73 All the children (<u>are</u>, is) having a hamburger. ✓

74 Which one of you three (<u>are</u>, is) going to do it? ✗

75 How many of you (<u>are</u>, is) eleven years old? ✓

③ 6

Fill each blank with an **adjective** based on the name of a country.

76 _____ *The Welsh* lamb comes from Wales. ✓

77 _____ *Tibetan* rugs are made in Tibet. ✓

78 Holland is the home of the _____ *Dutch* people. ✓

79 _____ *Portuguese* people come from Portugal. ✓

④ 4

Copy and punctuate the passage correctly, without affecting lower case or capital letters.

80–92 Jacob was beginning to get worried he hadn't heard them for at least five minutes Jacob called Is that you Sandy Please answer if it is.

Of course it is Who else would it be responded Sandy giggling ·

_____

_____

_____

_____

_____

_____

Complete the table.

93–100

No. of syllables	Word		
3	Banana	tomato	cucumber
4	satisfaction	everlasting	
5	dissatisfaction		

A powerful enchanter in the guise of a crocodile, on winning a game of heads or tails against King Merrion the Carefree, requested as his prize all the dark in the King's kingdom. This he was granted but it had a devastating effect. The princess and her greatest friend the horse called Houniman decided to solve the predicament that King Merrion had got them in …

The princess rode on Houniman and he galloped steadily northwards for seven days and what ought to have been seven nights, over a sea of ice, until they came to the Land of Everlasting Winter, where the words freeze as you speak them, and even thoughts rattle in your head like icicles.

There they found the Lord of Winter, in the form of a giant eagle, brooding on a rock.   5

'Sir,' called Gudrun from a good way off – for it was so cold in his neighbourhood that the very birds froze in the air and hung motionless – 'can you tell us where we can find a bit of dark?'

He lifted his head with its great hooked beak and gave them an angry look.

'Why should I help you? I have only one little piece of dark, and I am keeping it   10
for myself, under my wing, so that it may grow.'

'Does dark grow?' said Gudrun.

'Of course it grows, stupid girl! Cark! Be off with you!' And the eagle spread one wing (keeping the other tight folded) so that a great white flurry of snow and wind drove towards Gudrun and Houniman, and they turned and galloped away.   15

At the edge of the Land of Winter they saw an old woman leading a reindeer loaded with wood.

'Mother,' called Gudrun, 'can you tell us where we might find a bit of dark?'

'Give me a piece of bread and cheese for myself and some corn for my beast and I will consider.'   20

So they gave her the bread and corn and she considered. Presently she said:

'There will be plenty of dark in the past. You should go to No Man's Land, the frontier where the present slips into the past, and perhaps you might be able to pick up a bit of dark there.'

'Good,' said the princess, 'that sounds hopeful. But in which direction does the past lie?'   25

'Towards the setting sun, of course!' snapped the old woman, and she gave her reindeer a thump to make it jog along faster.

So Gudrun and Houniman turned towards the setting sun and galloped on for seven days and what should have been seven nights, until they reached No Man's Land. This was a strange and misty region, with low hills and marshes; in the middle of it they came   30
to a great lake, on the shore of which sat an old poet in a little garden of cranberry shrubs. Instead of water the lake was filled with blue-grey mist, and the old poet was drawing out the mist in long threads, and twisting them and turning them into poems. It was very silent all around there, with not a living creature, and the old poet was so absorbed in what he did that he never lifted his head until they stood beside him.   35

'Can you tell us, uncle poet,' said Gudrun, 'where we might pick up a bit of dark?'

'Dark?' he said absently. 'Eh, what's that? You want a bit of dark? There's plenty at the bottom of the lake.'

So Gudrun dismounted and walked to the edge of the lake, and looked down through the mist. Thicker and thicker it grew, darker and darker, down in the depths   40 of the lake, and as she looked down she could see all manner of strange shapes, and some that seemed familiar too – faces that she had once known, places that she had once visited, all sunk down in the dark depths of the past. As she leaned over, the mist seemed to rise up around her, so that she began to become sleepy, to forget who she was and what she had come for…   45

'Gudrun! Come back!' cried Houniman loudly, and he stretched out his long neck and caught hold of her by the hair and pulled her back, just as she was about to topple into the lake.

'Climb on my back and let's get out of here!' he said. 'Dark or no dark, this place is too dangerous!'   50

But Gudrun cried to the poet, 'Uncle poet, isn't there any other place where we might pick up a bit of dark?'

'Dark?' he said. 'You want a bit of dark? Well, I suppose you might try the Gates of Death; dark grows around there.'

The Cost of Night by Joan Aiken

Answer these questions.

1 Where do words freeze as you speak?

_____

2 Which animal was the Lord of Winter? _____

3 What is the princess's name? _____

4 What are Houniman and the princess looking for?

_____

5 Find an **onomatopoeic** word used by the Lord of Winter. _____

6 Where does the present slip into the past?

_____

7 Why do Gudrun and Houniman gallop for 'what should have been seven nights' (line 29)?

_____

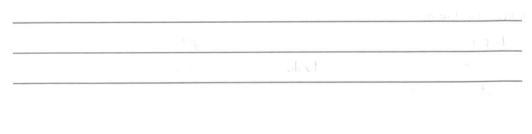

8–9 Describe in your own words how Gudrun felt at the edge of the lake. Use evidence from the passage to support your answer.

_____

_____

_____

10 What did Houniman mean when he said, 'Dark or no dark, this place is too dangerous' (lines 49–50)?

_____

11 The title of this story is 'The Cost of Night'. Why do you think it is called this?

_____

12–15 The princess and Houniman meet three characters in this passage. Describe briefly each character they meet and make a note of something they all have in common.

_____

_____

_____

_____

16–20 Describe five events or features of the story that make it a fable.

_____

_____

_____

_____

_____

◯ 20

Write a word, beginning with *a*, which has the same meaning as the word on the left.

21 stick	ad_____	**22** quicken	ac_____
23 leave	ab_____	**24** sharp	ac_____
25 change	al_____	**26** plentiful	ab_____
27 shorten	ab_____	**28** try	at_____

D 9

◯ 8

Put these words in the correct columns.

29–40

happy	energy	expect	caught	met
uncertainty	drown	foolish	sunlight	reality
carefree	artificial			

D 6

45

Nouns	Verbs	Adjectives

12

Write an **antonym** for each word by adding a **prefix**.

D 9
E 2

41 patient _____   42 legible _____

43 responsible _____   44 contented _____

45 informed _____   46 sense _____

47 considerate _____   48 certain _____

8

Add the missing commas to the passage.

D 4

49–55 As the water trickled off the roof on to the path and down into the ever increasing stream Mark wished it would stop raining. Usually a patient boy he wouldn't have minded being trapped in the club house if he wasn't supposed to have been home ages ago. Mark had left with Tony Matt Anil and Rick but had to return as he had forgotten in all the excitement his football kit.

7

Write the **plural** form of each of these words.

E 2

56 dynasty _____   57 survey _____

58 frequency _____   59 injury _____

60 gallery _____   61 melody _____

62 anthology _____   63 photocopy _____

8

Add the missing semicolons and commas to these **sentences**.

D 4
D 5

64–66 The young cat full of fun killed the mouse Dad was pleased.

67 The aircraft was nearly empty empty seats are good for passengers but bad news for airlines.

68 Polar bears are beginning to move closer to people's homes it can't be long before there is an attack.

69–71 Rugby training is hard work we start with a run continue with 30 press-ups practise moves and finish with a training match.

8

State whether each of these **sentences** has an **active** or **passive verb**.

D 6

72 Brian washed the dishes. _____

73 Janie wrote her diary. _____

74 The cyclist was struck by the lorry. _____

75 Columbus reached America in 1492. _____

76 The moon was first visited by Neil Armstrong. _____

5

Explain what each of these **metaphors** means.

E 2

77 The sky was on fire.

_____

78 The moon was a ghostly galleon.

_____

79 The birds were a joyful choir.

_____

80 The thunder is an angry giant.

_____

81 The clouds were cotton wool.

_____

82 The sea was an angry dog.

_____

6

Circle the unstressed vowels.

E 2

83 silently	84 prison	85 dictionary
86 nursery	87 company	88 chocolate
89 different	90 fragrance	91 temperature

9

Complete each of these **conditional sentences**.

D 1
D 6

92 Sundeep will go to the shop _____

93 The battery in your mobile phone will run out _____

_____

94 We might go to the cinema _____

_____

3

E 2

Underline the correct word in brackets.

95 Has Keith or Kim the (good, better, best) bat?

96 Of all the children he was the (late, later, latest) to arrive.

97 The more sweets you eat the (bad, worse, worst) your teeth will be.

98 The (little, less, least) you can expect is to receive a letter.

99–100 The (hard, harder, hardest) you work the (clever, cleverer, cleverest) you will be.

6

Now go to the Progress Chart to record your score! **Total** 100

Paper 9

B

The room in which the boys were fed, was a large stone hall, with a copper at one end: out of which the master, dressed in an apron for the purpose, and assisted by one or two women, ladled the gruel at meal-times. Of this festive composition each boy had one porringer, and no more – except on occasions of great public rejoicing, when he had two ounces and a quarter of bread besides. The bowls never wanted washing. The boys polished them with their spoons till they shone again; and when they had performed this operation (which never took very long, the spoons being nearly as large as the bowls), they would sit staring at the copper, with such eager eyes, as if they could have devoured the very bricks of which it was

5

composed; employing themselves, meanwhile, in sucking their fingers most assiduously, with the view of catching up any stray splashes of gruel that might have been cast thereon. Boys have generally excellent appetites. Oliver Twist and his companions suffered the tortures of slow starvation for three months: at last they got so voracious and wild with hunger, that one boy, who was tall for his age, and hadn't been used to that sort of thing (for his father had kept a small cookshop), hinted darkly to his companions, that unless he had another basin of gruel *per diem,* he was afraid he might some night happen to eat the boy who slept next to him, who happened to be a weakly youth of tender age. He had a wild, hungry eye; and they implicitly believed him. A council was held; lots were cast who should walk up to the master after supper that evening, and ask for more; and it fell to Oliver Twist.

The evening arrived; the boys took their places. The master, in his cook's uniform, stationed himself at the copper; his pauper assistants ranged themselves behind him; the gruel was served out; and a long grace was said over the short commons. The gruel disappeared; the boys whispered to each other, and winked at Oliver; while his next neighbours nudged him. Child as he was, he was desperate with hunger, and reckless with misery. He rose from the table; and advancing to the master, basin and spoon in hand, said, somewhat alarmed at his own temerity:

'Please, sir, I want some more.'

The master was a fat, healthy man; but he turned very pale. He gazed in stupefied astonishment on the small rebel for some seconds, and then clung for support to the copper. The assistants were paralysed with wonder; the boys with fear.

'What!' said the master at length, in a faint voice.

'Please, sir,' replied Oliver, 'I want some more.'

The master aimed a blow at Oliver's head with the ladle, pinioned him in his arms, and shrieked aloud for the beadle.

The board were sitting in solemn conclave, when Mr Bumble rushed into the room in great excitement, and addressing the gentleman in the high chair, said,

'Mr Limbkins, I beg your pardon, sir! Oliver Twist has asked for more!' There was a general start. Horror was depicted on every countenance.

'For *more*!' said Mr Limbkins. 'Compose yourself, Bumble, and answer me distinctly. Do I understand that he asked for more, after he had eaten the supper allotted by the dietary?'

'He did, sir,' replied Bumble.

'That boy will be hung,' said the gentleman in the white waistcoat; 'I know that boy will be hung.'

Nobody controverted the prophetic gentleman's opinion. An animated discussion took place. Oliver was ordered into instant confinement; and a bill was next morning pasted on the outside of the gate, offering a reward of five pounds to anybody who would take Oliver Twist off the hands of the parish. In other words, five pounds and Oliver Twist were offered to any man or woman who wanted an apprentice to any trade, business, or calling.

'I never was more convinced of anything in my life,' said the gentleman in the white waistcoat, as he knocked at the gate and read the bill next morning: 'I never was more convinced of anything in my life, than I am that that boy will come to be hung.'...

For a week after the commission of the impious and profane offence of asking for more, Oliver remained a close prisoner in the dark and solitary room to which he had been consigned by the wisdom and mercy of the board. It appears, at first

sight, not unreasonable to suppose, that, if he had entertained a becoming feeling
of respect for the prediction of the gentleman in the white waistcoat, he would have   *60*
established that sage individual's prophetic character, once and forever, by tying
one end of his pocket-handkerchief to a hook in the wall, and attaching himself to
the other. To the performance of this feat, however, there was one obstacle: namely,
that pocket-handkerchiefs being decided articles of luxury, had been, for all future
times and ages, removed from the noses of paupers by the express order of the   *65*
board, in council assembled; solemnly given and pronounced under their hands
and seals. There was still greater obstacle in Oliver's youth and childishness. He
only cried bitterly all day; and, when the long, dismal night came on, spread his little
hands before his eyes to shut out the darkness, and crouching in the corner, tried to
sleep: ever and anon waking with a start and a tremble, and drawing himself closer   *70*
and closer to the wall, as if to feel even its cold hard surface were a protection in
the gloom and loneliness which surrounded him.

From *Oliver Twist* by Charles Dickens

Answer these questions.

1 When were the boys given bread?

_____

2 For how long had the boys been starving?

_____

3 Find another word in the passage for 'a bowl'. _____

4 Why did the boys suck their fingers?

_____

5 What is meant by 'A council was held' (line 19)?

_____

6–7 Why was it decided someone should ask for more food? How was Oliver
chosen?

_____

_____

8 Oliver is described as 'reckless with misery' (line 26). What does this mean?

_____

_____

9 Write a definition for the word 'temerity' (line 27).

_____

10 What does the description 'The master was a fat, healthy man' (line 29) emphasise in the context of the dining hall?

_____

_____

11–13 Describe Mr Bumble. Use evidence from the passage to support your answer.

_____

_____

_____

14–15 In your own words, describe the room in which Oliver was imprisoned.

_____

_____

16 What is suggested that Oliver could do with a pocket-handkerchief?

_____

17–18 How does the last sentence of the passage make you feel? Use evidence from the passage to support your answer.

_____

_____

19–20 Do you think Oliver's punishment was appropriate for the crime he committed? What does this tell you about those who carried out the punishment?

_____

_____

20

D 6

From each of the words in bold make an **adjective** to fit the **sentence**.

21 anxiety   The _____ woman waited for his return.

22 peril   The mountaineers set out on their _____ climb.

23 region   They heard the report on the _____ news.

24 choir   The _____ society performed at the concert.

25 method   They tackled the task in a very _____ way.

26 length   Her _____ dress was much admired.

27 ornament   The _____ gate was painted white.

28 metal   It made a _____ noise when it fell to the ground.

8

E 2

Complete these **similes**.

29 Like water off a _____.

30 Like a bull in a _____.

31 As fit as a _____.

32 As mad as a _____.

33 As poor as a _____.

34 As dead as a _____.

6

E 2

Use the words in bold to fill the gaps.

sauce	**practice**	**desert**	**alter**	**stationary**
source	**practise**	**dessert**	**altar**	**stationery**

35 We all like apple _____ with pork.

36 There were beautiful lilies on the _____.

37 The _____ of the River Dee is in North Wales.

38 I must do some _____.

39 The train was _____; they need not have hurried.

40 The team must _____ their bowling.

41 Miss Bell must _____ her timetable.

42 The Sahara _____ is in Africa.

43 "You will need more _____ to write all those letters."

44 We had peaches and cream for our _____.

10

D 2

Make the **sentences** more interesting by adding a **clause** to each of them.

45 My friend knows more about horses than I do.

_____

_____

46 My Uncle Matt is coming to stay.

_____

_____

47 We enjoyed the band at the wedding.

_____

_____

48 Harry swam thirty-six lengths of the school pool.

_____

_____

49 I love going out on my bike.

_____

_____

50 This year we are going on holiday to France.

_____

_____

6

E 2

Write the modern version of each of the following words.

51 hath _____ **52** shouldst _____

53 cometh _____ **54** hither _____

55 art _____ **56** wilt _____

57 saith _____ **58** shalt _____

8

D 5

Add the missing apostrophes.

59 the cats tail **60** the five childrens coats

61 the apples pips **62** the three dogs bones

63 the seven houses keys **64** the videos case

65 the four horses foals **66** the six computers keyboards

8

Add the missing **collective nouns**.

67 A _____ of cattle.

68 A _____ of insects.

69 A _____ of lions.

70 A _____ of musicians.

71 A _____ of puppies.

72 A _____ of sheep.

73 A _____ of crows.

Add the **suffix** *ship* or *ment* to each of these words.

74–81	engage	align	member	receiver	censor
	scholar	enhance	content		

_____   _____   _____

_____   _____   _____

_____   _____

Rewrite the passage, separating the words correctly and adding the missing capital letters and punctuation.

82–96 itwassundayafternoonthesunwasglintingthroughthetreesanditwaswarm
ameliacalledtogeorgearewegoingtodosomethingtodayi'mboredofjustsitting
hereheignoredher

_____

_____

_____

_____

_____

_____

Make up your own **mnemonic** for each of these words.

E 2

97 weight _____

98 concentration _____

99 permanent _____

100 unfortunately _____

4

Now go to the Progress Chart to record your score!   Total ◯ 100

Paper 10

B

Victoria (r. 1837–1901)

Queen Victoria maintained a detailed diary, her famous Journal, which is contained in 111 large manuscript volumes. These volumes constitute about a third of the original, as her diaries were edited after her death by her youngest daughter Princess Beatrice, at Queen Victoria's request.

On William IV's death, and her accession aged 18 years: Tuesday, 20 June 1837 at Kensington Palace

I was awoke at 6 o'clock by Mamma, who told me that the Archbishop of
Canterbury and Lord Conyngham were here, and wished to see me. I got out of
bed and went into my sitting-room (only in my dressing-gown), and *alone*, and saw
them. Lord Conyngham (the Lord Chamberlain) then acquainted me that my poor
Uncle, the King, was no more, and had expired at 12 minutes past 2 this   5
morning, and consequently that I am *Queen*. Lord Conyngham knelt down and
kissed my hand, at the same time delivering to me the official announcement of
the poor King's demise. The Archbishop then told me that the Queen was desirous
that he should come and tell me the details of the last moments of my poor, good
Uncle; he said that he had directed his mind to religion, and had died in a perfectly   10
happy, quiet state of mind, and was quite prepared for his death. He added that
the King's sufferings at the last were not very great but that there was a good
deal of uneasiness. Lord Conyngham, whom I charged to express my feelings of
condolence and sorrow to the poor Queen, returned directly to Windsor. I then went
to my room and dressed.   15
    Since it has pleased Providence to place me in this station, I shall do my utmost
to fulfil my duty towards my country; I am very young and perhaps in many, though
not in all things, inexperienced, but I am sure, that very few have more real good
will and more real desire to do what is fit and right than I have ...

At 9 came Lord Melbourne, whom I saw in my room, and of COURSE *quite* 20
ALONE as I shall *always* do all my Ministers. He kissed my hand and I then
acquainted him that it had long been my intention to retain him and the rest of the
present Ministry at the head of affairs, and that it could not be in better hands than
his ... He then read to me the Declaration which I was to read to the Council, which
he wrote himself and which is a very fine one. I then talked with him some little 25
longer time after which he left me ... I like him very much and feel confidence in
him. He is a very straightforward, honest, clever and good man. I then wrote a letter
to the Queen ...

Coronation: Thursday, 28 June 1838

I was awoke at four o'clock by the guns in the Park, and could not get much sleep 30
afterwards on account of the noise of the people, bands, etc. Got up at 7 feeling
strong and well; the Park presented a curious spectacle; crowds of people up
to Constitution Hill, soldiers, bands, etc. I dressed, having taken a little breakfast
before I dressed, and a little after. At half past 9 I went into the next room dressed
exactly in my House of Lords costume ... At 10 I got into the State Coach with the 35
Duchess of Sutherland and Lord Albemarle, and we began our progress.

It was a fine day, and the crowds of people exceeded what I have ever seen;
many as there were the day I went to the City, it was nothing – nothing to the
multitudes, the millions of my loyal subjects who were assembled in *every* spot to
witness the Procession. Their good humour and excessive loyalty was beyond 40
everything, and I really cannot say *how* proud I feel to be the Queen of *such* a
Nation. I was alarmed at times for fear that the people would be crushed and
squeezed on account of the tremendous rush and pressure.

I reached the Abbey (Westminster) amid deafening cheers at a little after half past
11; I first went into a robing-room quite close to the entrance, where I found 45
my eight Train-bearers – all dressed alike and beautifully, in white satin and silver
tissue, with wreaths of silver corn-ears in front, and a small one of pink roses round
the plait behind, and pink roses in the trimming of the dresses. After putting on my
Mantle, and the young ladies having properly got hold of it, and Lord Conyngham
holding the end of it, I left the robing-room and the Procession began. The sight 50
was splendid; the bank of Peeresses quite beautiful, all in their robes, and the
Peers on the other side. My young Train-bearers were always near me, and helped
whenever I wanted anything. The Bishop of Durham stood on one side near me.

At the beginning of the Anthem ... I retired to St Edward's Chapel, a small dark
place immediately behind the Altar, with my Ladies and Train-bearers; took off my 55
crimson robe and kirtle and put on the Supertunica of Cloth of Gold, also in the
shape of a kirtle, which was put over a singular sort of little gown of linen trimmed
with lace; I also took off my circlet of diamonds, and then proceeded bare-headed
into the Abbey; I was then seated upon St Edward's chair where the Dalmatic robe
was clasped round me by the Lord Great Chamberlain. Then followed all the 60
various things; and last (of those things) the Crown being placed on my head;
– which was, I must own, a most beautiful impressive moment; *all* the Peers and
Peeresses put on their Coronets at the same instant ... The shouts, which were
very great, the drums, the trumpets, the firing of the guns, all at the same instant,
rendered the spectacle most imposing. 65

... the Procession being formed, I replaced my Crown (which I had taken off for
a few minutes), took the Orb in my left hand and the Sceptre in my right, and thus

loaded proceeded through the Abbey, which resounded with cheers ... At about half past 4 I re-entered my carriage, the Crown on my head and Sceptre and Orb in my hand, and we proceeded the same way as we came – the crowds if possible having increased. The enthusiasm, affection and loyalty was really touching, and I shall ever remember this day as the proudest of my life. I came home at a little after 6, – really *not* feeling tired.

... I then sat on the sofa for a little while ... Mamma ... remained to see the Illuminations, and only came in later ... I said to Lord Melbourne when I first sat down, I felt a little tired on my feet ... Spoke of the weight of the robes etc. and he turned round to me and said *so* kindly, 'And you did it beautifully, – every part of it, with so much taste; it's a thing that you can't give a person advice upon; it must be left to a person.' ... Stayed in the drawing-room till 20 minutes past 11, but remained till 12 o'clock on Mamma's balcony looking at the fireworks in Green Park, which were quite beautiful.

From The British Monarchy web site [http://www.royal.gov.uk]

Answer these questions.

1 Who edited Queen Victoria's diaries after her death?

_____

2 Where did Victoria hear of the King's death?

_____

3 What relation was the King to Victoria? _____

4–5 Give the meaning of the following words as they are used in the extracts:

desirous (line 8) _____

condolence (line 14) _____

6–7 Describe in your own words Victoria's first thoughts on becoming Queen.

_____

_____

8–9 Victoria wrote a letter to the Queen. What do you think she might have included in it? Use evidence from the extract to support your answer.

_____

_____

10 How long after hearing about the King's death was Victoria crowned?

_____

11–12 Victoria awoke at four o'clock on the morning of her Coronation. She states she 'could not get much sleep afterwards on account of the noise of the people, bands, etc.'. What else do you think might have kept her awake?

_____

_____

13 Why, on lines 58–59, did Victoria proceed 'bare-headed into the Abbey'?

_____

14 Why do you think the young Queen Victoria described herself as '_loaded_', on line 68?

_____

15 In addition to the Crown, name one other object that was given to the new Queen during the ceremony.

_____

16–17 Give two reasons why so many people gathered to watch the Queen go by.

_____

_____

18–20 Using evidence from the diary extracts, describe in your own words how Victoria felt at her Coronation.

_____

_____

_____

20

Underline the word on each line which has the same meaning as the word in bold, and ring the word which has the opposite meaning.

D 9

21–22 blame	wrong	careless	censure	bad	praise
23–24 elevate	high	raise	lower	elude	bottom
25–26 assemble	disperse	divide	together	unite	gather
27–28 expand	larger	contract	smaller	increase	disband
29–30 least	little	most	minimum	lot	more

10

Add a different **conjunction** to complete each **sentence**.

D 6

31 I intend to go _____ you like it or not.

32 We had to wait in the rain _____ the bus came.

33 You won't finish your drawing _____ you hurry up.

34 You must make the cake _____ it is your party.

4

E 2

Each of these words has a missing silent letter. Rewrite each word with its missing letter.

35 rythm	_____	36 rein	_____
37 not	_____	38 rombus	_____
39 colum	_____	40 our	_____
41 hym	_____	42 gard	_____

8

D 6

State whether each of these sentences has an **active** or **passive verb**.

43 The dog eats his bone.   _____

44 The ice-cream will be eaten by Grandad.   _____

45 Jess swam thirty lengths of the pool.   _____

46 The car crashed into the lamp post.   _____

47 Rudi caught the thief.   _____

48 The bill will be paid by Uncle Rick.   _____

49 Alice was taken to the cinema by her parents.   _____

7

E 2

Match each word with its **definition** in bold by writing the correct number in the space.

(1) **hermit**   (2) **moisture**   (3) **frighten**   (4) **nearby**

(5) **dregs**   (6) **sitting**   (7) **enemy**   (8) **responsible**

50 intimidate	____	51 sedentary	____
52 sediment	____	53 humidity	____
54 adversary	____	55 liable	____
56 recluse	____	57 adjacent	____

8

Write a statement and a question that include the words in bold.

D 1

58–59 **Peter   homework**

Statement _____

Question _____

60–61 **sailing   France   holiday**

Statement _____

Question _____

62–63 **photograph   class   yesterday**

Statement _____

Question _____

64–65 **chickenpox   bed   infectious**

Statement _____

Question _____

8

E 2

Write what you think each **prefix** means and then write a word with each **prefix**.

e.g. **bi** =   *two*   *bicycle*

66–67 **tele** =   _____   _____

68–69 **micro** =   _____   _____

70–71 **sub** =   _____   _____

72–73 **aqua** =   _____   _____

74–75 **auto** =   _____   _____

10

D 6

Underline the **prepositions** in the following **sentences**.

76 His book is different from mine.

77 Mrs Trueman is an authority on beetles.

78 That is an exception to the rule.

79 They were not allowed beyond the fence.

80 The drink spilt on the table.

81 Susie saw the strange man outside her window.

82 The fireman raced up the ladder to save the child.

7

Write four sentences, each with a colon. In two of the sentences use the colon to introduce a quotation and in the other two to introduce a list.

D 1
D 5

83 _____

_____

_____

84 _____

_____

_____

85 _____

_____

_____

86 _____

_____

_____

4

D 6

Write the simple **past tense** of these **verbs**.

87 to fight	_____	88 to build	_____
89 to run	_____	90 to get	_____
91 to mean	_____	92 to become	_____
93 to find	_____	94 to feel	_____

8

E 2

Rewrite these words correctly.

95 intresting	_____	96 unfortuntely	_____
97 specfication	_____	98 infrstructure	_____
99 rehersal	_____	100 indepndence	_____

6

Now go to the Progress Chart to record your score!   Total   100

Progress Chart   Fifth Papers in English

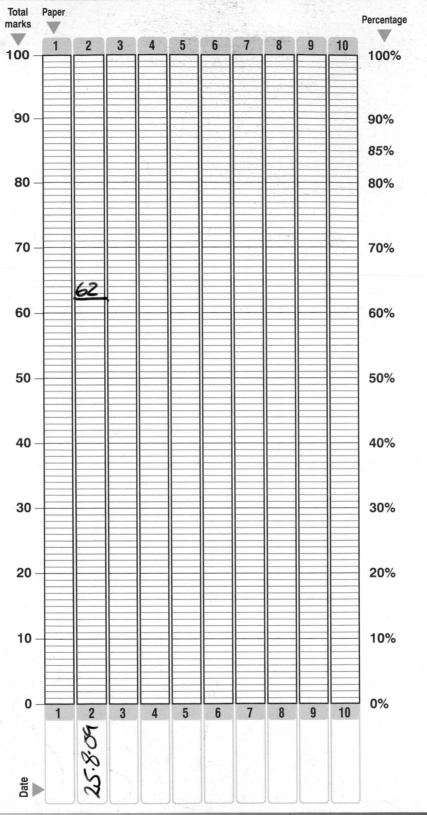

Total marks ▼   Paper ▼

Percentage ▼

| Paper | 1 | 2 | 3 | 4 | 5 | 6 | 7 | 8 | 9 | 10 |

100 — 100%

90 — 90%
— 85%
80 — 80%

70 — 70%

62

60 — 60%

50 — 50%

40 — 40%

30 — 30%

20 — 20%

10 — 10%

0 — 0%

| Date ▶ | 1 | 2 | 3 | 4 | 5 | 6 | 7 | 8 | 9 | 10 |
| | | 25.8.09 | | | | | | | | |

When you've finished the book use the Next Step Planner ▶